JONÁS SUFURINO

La Magia Suprema

Negra, Roja e Infernal

DE LOS

CALDEOS Y DE LOS EGIPCIOS

traducida, compilada y comentada, con sujeción al texto hebreo

POR EL

DOCTOR MOORNE

ROMA, MCMXVI

THE SUPREME BLACK, RED AND INFERNAL MAGIC OF THE CHALDEANS AND
EGYPTIANS
First published in 1916 as *La Magia Suprema: Negra, Roja e Infernal de los
Caldeos y de los Egipcio* by the World Occult Society.
Attributed to Jonas Sufurino, translated, compiled and commented, subject
to the Hebrew text, by Doctor Moorne.
Translated from the Spanish and with a new introduction by Steve
Savedow, translation copyright © 2022.
Cover image: Frontispiece from Libro de San Cipriano: Libro Completo
de Verdadera Hechicero, Casa Editorial Maucci, 1905.
Interior images are from the original edition and are in the public domain.
Title page shows the original cover of *La Magia Suprema.*
Published by Hadean Press, West Yorkshire.
All Rights Reserved Worldwide.

ISBN 978-1-914166-26-6 (HB)
ISBN 978-1-914166-27-3 (PB)

Hardcover edition printed by Biddles, Norfolk.
First published in 2022.
Hadean Press
West Yorkshire
England
www.hadeanpress.com

This work has been published for its historical value. The publisher does
not not endorse nor condone the use of the recipes in this book. See your
physician if you need medical attention.

The Supreme

Black, Red and Infernal Magic

OF THE

Chaldeans and Egyptians

BY THE MONK

Jonás Sufurino

APPENDIX TO THE GRIMOIRE OF SAINT CYPRIAN

TRANSLATED BY

Steve Savedow

This book is fondly dedicated to the future of my young twins, Daniel Barry and Jessica Belle Savedow.

Contents

New Introduction

THIS BOOK was published in Rome in 1916; it is quite scarce, and is an interesting and obscure little grimoire text which for some reason has not previously been translated into English. The original editor, in his introduction, claims the material is drawn from previously withheld writings that were not included in the classic Spanish edition of the *Libro de San Cipriano*, a rather popular occult/magical work.

Libro de San Cipriano

LIBRO COMPLETO DE VERDADERA MAGIA
O SEA

TESORO DEL HECHICERO
ESCRITO EN ANTIGUOS PERGAMINOS HEBREOS, ENTREGADOS POR
LOS ESPÍRITUS AL MONJE ALEMÁN

JONAS SUFURINO
CONTIENE:

La Clavícula de Salomón, Invocaciones, Pactos, Exorcismos,
El Dragón Rojo y La Cabra Infernal,
La Gallina Negra, Escuela de Sortilegios, El Gran Grimorio
o El Pacto de la Sangre
Candela Mágica para descubrir encantamientos,
Recopilación de la Magia caldea y egipcia, Filtros,
Encantamientos, Hechicerías y Sortilegios

Nueva edición ilustrada

CASA EDITORIAL MAUCCI
Gran medalla en las Exposiciones de Viena de 1903, Madrid 1907, Budapest 1907
y gran premio en la de Buenos Aires 1910
Calle de Mallorca, 166.—BARCELONA

It is now known that the editor, 'Dr. Moorne', was actually Franscisco Moreno (1852–1919). Born in Buenos Aires (a lifelong citizen), he was a prominent, respected Argentinian anthropologist and scientist, who apparently kept his occult interests secret, which is understandable considering the attitudes of the time in which he lived. Dr. Moorne mentions, in his foreword to this text, that the release of the Spanish St. Cyprian grimoire was so successful that he was encouraged to publish the "reserved matter" that was left out of the original book. He referred to this text, which is approximately 160 pages in softcover format, as an "Appendix" to the original.

There have been several different English editions of the infamous *Book of Saint Cyprian* published; to name a few:

The Book of St. Cyprian: The Sorcerer's Treasure by José Leitão (Hadean Press, 2014)

The Testament of Cyprian the Mage: Comprehending the Book of Saint Cyprian & His Magical Elements and an Elucidation of the Testament of Solomon (Encyclopaedia Goetica, Volume III) by Jake Stratton-Kent (Scarlet Imprint, 2014)

The Grimoire of St. Cyprian: Clavis Inferni by Stephen Skinner & David Rankine (Golden Hoard Press, 2017)

The Book of St. Cyprian: The Great Book of True Magic by Humberto Maggi (Nephilim Press, 2018)

The Grimoire of St. Cyprian, English Edition by Edmund Kelly (Lulu Publications, 2019)

These listed are English translations or examinations of various versions of the legendary grimoire published just in the past decade, based on a variety of manuscripts and printed texts, but over the centuries there have also been numerous other titles on the subject of Saint Cyprian of Antioch (d. 304?),[1] taken from both his own writings and biographical works by others, which detail his life and times, his conversion to Christianity encouraged by Saint Justina, and his interest in magic, occultism, and dealings with the devil or demons. Some of the earliest known references

---

1 Who is not to be confused with Saint Cyprian of Carthage or Caecilius (210–258).

to Cyprian's grimoire are in the *Three Books of Occult Philosophy* of Henry Cornelius Agrippa (1486–1535).

The Skinner and Rankine text is based on the very attractive manuscript Wellcome 2000, fully titled *The Key of Hell with White and Black Magic as Proven by Metatron*, a mixture of Greek, Hebrew, and Latin. Also included is an extensive, fully detailed biographical and bibliographical introduction. José Leitão's book is drawn from the Portuguese version, and the Maggi and Kelly works are both taken from Spanish editions.

The specific Spanish edition which is most often referenced in the present text was first published in the early twentieth century as *Libro de San Cipriano*,[2] (*Libro de San Cipriano – Libro Completo de Verdadera Magia O Sea Tesoro Del Hechicero; Escrito en Antiguos Pergaminos Hebreos, Entregados Por Los Espíritus Al Monje Aleman Jonas Sufurino*, Nueva edicion illustrada: Casa Editorial Maucci, Calle de Mallorca, 166, Barcelona; translated as: *Book of Saint Cyprian – Complete Book of True Magic, or The Sorcerer's Treasure; Written in Ancient Hebrew Scrolls, Given by the Spirits to the German Monk, Jonas Sufurino*, New Illustrated Edition: Maucci Publishing House, 166 Mallorca Street, Barcelona) and was attributed to the legendary German monk Jonas Sufurino (also Sulfurino, Surfurino) of the tenth century. There are a scarce few references to this monk in recent texts, most of which include the same small bit of information which is detailed here:

"One late nineteenth-century Spanish grimoire, for instance, related how in the year 1001 a German monk named Jonas Sufurino, librarian of the monastery of Brooken, conjured up the Devil on a mountaintop one night and was given a copy of

---

2 The text includes versions of the *Key of Solomon, Grand Grimoire, La Cabre Infernal, El Pacto de la Sangre*, plus several others. See <http://iapsop.com/ssoc/1905__sufurino___libro_de_san_cipriano_verdadera_magia.pdf>.

Cyprian's magic book as reward."[3]... "As early as 1916 a limited edition Solomonic work entitled *La Magia Suprema Negra* was produced [in Bueno Aires], though its stated place of publication was Rome. Its equally spurious author was the legendary tenth-century monk Jonas Sufurino, finder of the *Libro de San Cypriano*. The man who supposedly translated it from German and edited it was the mysterious Dr. Moorne. An early-twentieth-century catalogue of cheap occult publications produced by the Madrid publishers Libreria de Pueyo shows that Dr. Moorne was cited as the translator of a raft of cheap magic books at the time...".[4]

And also in this promotional quote from the recent paperback Spanish edition of *La Magia Suprema* attributed to Sufurino, published in Puerto Rico:

"It was published in Rome in 1916 by the World Occult Society. Grimoires like this gave way to various modern movements such as Wicca, Neo-Satanism, and Chaos magic. ... This work alludes as its author to Jonas Sufurino, a German monk from the monastery of Brocken. In the year 1001, the legend tells us that this monk, seeking knowledge, invoked Lucifer himself, who presented himself to him and agreed to give him what he asked for, that he would reveal all the secrets of this world and of the others. Lucifer also told him that he would give him a book that would be like the catechism of the secret sciences, a catechism that only the initiated could understand. When the time came, Lucifer handed over a book written in Hebrew on virgin parchment, the same one that Cipriano the magician had. When delivering this

---

3 Owen Davies, *Grimoires: A History of Magic Books* (Oxford: Oxford University Press, 2009), p. 33.

4 Davies, *Grimoires*, p. 245.

book, Lucifer indicated to the monk that he would never depart from it and it could not be destroyed in any way."[5]

Dr. Moorne appears to have taken it upon himself to apply the name of Sufurino as the 'author' of both the *San Cypriano* text as well as this book, *La Magia Suprema, Negra, Roja e Infernal, de los Caldeos y de los Egipcios*, using the name of Jonas Sufurino in bold print on both the cover and title page, attributing both texts to the legendary Monk of Brocken. While the legend is quite intriguing, I have the nagging suspicion that Moorne may have used the name as a selling point for the book (although I may be wrong about that). *La Magia Suprema* does seem to be of a later origin than the tenth century, or any other date of the medieval period. I must admit it is possible that Sufurino's name was mentioned in the original work to which Moorne referred, being a German manuscript derived from the Hebrew, although he never actually reveals the specific provenance of that manuscript.

José Leitão states in the introduction of his scholarly and comprehensive volume *The Book Of St. Cyprian: The Sorcerer's Treasure* that the Portuguese edition "is not so much an organized grimoire, existing in itself, but rather a large collection of purely oral and traditional folk magic traditions."[6] The Spanish edition is actually based on and influenced by the known classic and medieval grimoires, such as the *Grand Grimoire, Key of Solomon, Enchiridion of Pope Leo III, Heptameron* of Peter Abano, and others, and the same could be said about *La Magia Suprema*. The section on talismans displays a known Solomonic talisman, there is an exorcism prayer from the *Enchiridion*, and other conjurations

---

5 Jonas Sufurino, *La Magia Suprema de Jonás Sufurino*, ed. by Angel Rodriguez (San Juan: Editorial Nuevo Mundo, 2019); translation by the present author.

6 José Leitão, *The Book of St. Cyprian: The Sorcerer's Treasure* (France: Hadean Press, 2014), p. xxviii.

begin with evocations of Lucifer, Belzebuth, and Ashtaroth in the tradition of the *Grand Grimoire* and *Grimorium Verum*, to name just a few similarities. Also included is a selection of numerous charms and spells utilizing toads, bats, black cats, etc. for the purposes of acquiring love, protection against evil, making one's hair fall out, the evil eye, and many more. There are chapters on a variety of esoteric topics, including astrology, alchemy, numerology, cabala, gemstones, the mysteries of the Sphinx and Cleopatra (of beauty), and also unusual material involving the mysteries of virginity and virgin blood, the astral body, fluid larvae, elemental spirits, and more. It certainly appears to be more of a collection of works, rather than a specific singular grimoire text.

During my research, I had stumbled upon an interesting internet blog post entitled "Books of Saint Cyprian" by Félix Francisco Castro,[7] which offers a great amount of specific bibliographical information that readers may find of value. It also includes a photographic reproduction of the book cover of *El Libro Inferno*, which includes *El Libro de Cipriano* and *La Magia Suprema* in one volume, and also includes *Los Admirables Secretos Alberto El Grande*, or *Secrets of Albertus Magnus*, another popular nineteenth-century grimoire of folk magic. The copyright information basically mirrors the 1916 edition of the Cyprian grimoire noted above, attributed to Dr. Moorne and Sufurino.

While it appears that the *Libro de San Cipriano* is most certainly a nineteenth-century grimoire text, it is highly unlikely that it is related to the actual works of Saint Cyprian as advertised. However, it is still most worthy of study by the serious occultist and student of the magical arts as a collection of various hermetic subjects and ritual formulae. I am certain the reader will find great value in this work.

---

7 Translator's note: See: <https://danharms.wordpress.com/the-books-of-saint-cyprian/>.

A Necessary Explanation from the Publisher of This Book

WHEN, after many doubts and hesitations, we decided to undertake the publication of the work entitled BOOK OF SAINT CYPRIAN, *or* TREASURE OF THE SORCERER, we did not count on the extraordinary success that said work would achieve in the course of a very short time, success that we owe both to the goodness of the German original, in turn taken from the Hebrew, and in the translation of which we tried to be as scrupulous as possible, as well as to the favor that the public has given us by acquiring the work.

As the benevolent reader will recall very well, at the end of the aforementioned BOOK OF SAINT CYPRIAN and under the title of "Necessary Explanation", the translator of the work in question said that "some other matters were contained in the German original, but that it had not been possible to include them, as it deals with reserved matter".[8]

Now, encouraged by the success to which we have referred, and in the desire to defer to the numerous agitations that have been made to us, so that we may publish an APPENDIX TO THE BOOK OF SAINT CYPRIAN, in which these *other matters would be inserted that we considered as reserved matter*, we have decided to print that aforementioned APPENDIX, in which our readers will find, not only some extensions to *several of the subjects that are dealt with in*

---

8 We make this indication for those who know the first part of this treatise; for people who have not read it, we must recommend its acquisition, since it constitutes the first part of the present book.

Translator's note: This is, of course, a reference to the original Spanish edition mentioned above, previously published by Dr. Moorne.

*the book already mentioned several time*s, extensions that today we can present, by having stumbled upon a person who has managed to decipher the cabalistic words that the original[9] translator could not understand, but also the new and very interesting subjects to which we referred.

These subjects include: the way of making the magic ointments; how the pacts with the infernal spirits are broken; the enigma of the sphinx and the eight paradoxical questions with their respective answers; how men learned the magical arts; making philters and hexes; the complete art of dominating people; virtues and efficacy of virgin blood; secrets of the astral fire; how Simon the Magician was able to acquire the gift of impassivity and incombustibility, and, finally, several wonderful recipes for love and to cause or prevent the evil eye and all kinds of hexes.

Among the subjects of extension we also include some data on talismans, which we do not publish in the BOOK OF SAINT CYPRIAN, because we have not been able to decipher several of their cabalistic signs, something that has only been achieved after serious studies and a long time, and by force of self-denial and perseverance.

Among those matters of expansion are some very important, such as the Cabala; the Table of the Sephirot; a considerable part of Arithmancy, a treatise on numbers; many recipes on Alchemy, neither described nor dealt with in any of the books about this subject that have been published in Spanish; the Philosophy of Magic, and, ultimately, a large number of matters as rare as interesting.

Of the Cabala, we can say that of all the manuscripts and printed books that exist in Spain, even those not expurgated by the Inquisition, there is none that determined at all—as in this

---

9 Translator's note: "primitivo".

work it is done—the relationships that existed between the first magicians and the Creator of the Universe.

The origins of the supreme magic are described in this treatise, establishing the differences that exist between that which comes from the divine source, that is, that revealed by God and the heavenly spirits to perfect and chosen beings, and that transmitted by the rebellious angels to the children of men.

The table of the Sephirot and their opinions regarding the creation of worlds and created beings, is a completely new work in Spain, and that, therefore, deserves a careful and meticulous examination. Well studied, it will offer the key to mysteries that theology has not been able to explain to date.

You can also see in this treatise the enchantments produced by means of toads and by the fern seed, as well as the magic of beans, black cats, bats, etc.

With this Appendix that we publish today, surrendering ourselves completely to the benevolence of the public, and the BOOK OF SAINT CYPRIAN, which is its first and main part, we believe that the reader will find enough material to exercise the high black and red magic, as they did, all the great magicians, whose names fill the pages of the history of the planet which we inhabit.

Any doubt or hesitation about the matters contained in this book as well as that of SAINT CYPRIAN, or related to others that—we repeat—due to their great gravity and transcendence cannot be consigned in volumes that circulate from hand to hand, lest they could fall into those of some perverse and harmful beings, they will be answered verbally or by letter, for which we have the valuable assistance of a renowned professor of occult sciences.

The Editor[10]

---

10 Translator's note: Doctor Moorne, aka Francisco Moreno.

Part One

SUPREME RED MAGIC

Solomon and High Magic

Introduction

Solomon is the key to *post-flood* magic.[11] I, Cyprian, who have invoked him in my ecstasies, declare that the magic that the wise king wielded is true, and that true magic is nothing other than the principle of wisdom.

There are, however, two kinds of magic: black and red. The one, that exercised by the thaumaturges, endowed by the evil spirits with particular and exceptional faculties, and the other, which is exercised by the true magicians, revealed by Seth; by this transmitted to Noah, later spread throughout Chaldea by Abraham, to the Egyptian Priesthood by Joseph, ordered by Moses and practiced by Solomon, hidden under symbols in the *Old Testament*, revealed by Jesus to Saint John[12] and contained under hieratic figures in the Apocalypse of this apostle.

The first has been practiced by the sons of men, that is, by the descendants of Cain, and proceeds, according to the tradition of Enoch, from the rebellion of some angels, who by a similar sin[13] to that of Adam, were deprived of of grace. Those

---

11 Translator's note: "magia post-diluviana".

12 Translator's note: "San Juan".

13 Translator's note: "por un pecado analogo".

who practice thaumaturgia or this kind of magic are powerless to evoke the spirits of light. This magic involves the mastery of brute force; that is why Hermes Trismegistus, in his Emerald Tablet, represents her under the emblem of a tiger.

The second has been exercised by the children of God, by the descendants of Seth, and represents the sweetness of intelligence. It is exercised by those who have the same rule over the *macrocosm*[14] as over the *microcosm*,[15] because the will is humanly omnipotent when armed with the living forces of nature and with those of wisdom. The true magic comes from Seth, who by his virtues deserved to be initiated into it in Paradise itself, out of which his parents were cast by original sin. Hermes paints her under the emblem of a muffled ox at the feet of *Adda-Nari*, the Isis of the Indian people.[16]

The first magic represents rebellion; the second, obedience.

Do you want me to introduce you to the mysteries that Isis represents?

Well, see the engraving of her, examine it carefully and then read with great care, the description of those mysteries:

On her forehead is the sign of the *league* or of the universal generation.

On the right a tiger lies down on his feet; it is the evil or ignorant man; on the left, there is also curled up a muffled ox; it is the good man, the neophyte.

Isis stands between the evil and the good; between rebellion and obedience.

---

14 The *macrocosm* is the divine part of man when his soul reaches the state of complete purification.

15 *Microcosm* is the terrestrial body of the human being that, after death, contributes to the creation of new beings.

16 Translator's note: See Appendix for Levi's interpretation of this image.

ADDA-NARI
La Isis inda.

ADDA-NARI: ISIA INDA (DRAWING BY ELIPHAS LEVI, A.K.A. ALPHONSE LOUIS CONSTANT (1810–1875)

She has four arms that represent the four elements, each of which appears in her hands.

Fire is represented by a sword; the air by a ring; the earth by a branch in flower, which acts as a scepter; and the water by a cup.

A spring of milk flows from the head of Isis. It passes in front of the cloaked ox, falls at the foot of it and circulates around under the tiger, who does not see it.

The milk of science does not flow for the wicked. If he wants to drink it, he must see it, and to see it, he must bend his neck and look for it.

The two arms of Isis, on the side of the tiger, one holds the sword and the fire, the other the air and the ring. The air is the tempest.

The wicked one must be supported by fire and iron; the wicked must wear the ring; storms are raging over his head.

Nature is veiled by the part where the wicked one is.

The wicked one must know nothing; there must be no mercy for him.

Nature wears a necklace (or collar). On the side of the muffled ox, that necklace is made up of human heads, representing intelligence that joins intelligence and forms a divine chain; on the side of the wicked one, of the tiger, the necklace becomes iron chains.

Chains for the wicked one, prison, slavery, because the wicked one is a tiger; he is armed, he is strong, he loves blood and slaughter, and the sweet and useful ox must be protected against it.

The tiger looks suspiciously at the instruments of rigor suspended above his head, and remains immobile, sullen and restless.

On the part of the muffled ox, nature remains unveiled; for him there are no mysteries; for him the two arms of Isis support; one the flowering branch: it is the abundance, it is the intelligence that opens the bud of it, it is the palm, the scepter, the reward; the other, the cup that Isis brings to the spring from which the milk rises to calm the ox, to nourish it.

Two snakes that look at each other surround the arm with which Isis holds the blossoming branch: it is the symbol of balance, of the astral light, the secret of life.

Isis gives everything to the good; for him, she even offers the skin of the wicked, which she wears around her waist, on the side of the good.

And all the morality of this figure is summarized by a single sign: the hand that holds the blossoming branch makes the sign of esotericism, which recommends silence.

Esotericism is what must be hidden.

Exotericism is what is allowed to be said.[17]

The first three fingers are open, which in *palmistry* mean strength, power, and doom.

She hides the ring and the earpiece, which represent science and light.

All this implies saying to the good and the adepts: "Gather together and you will have the strength, the power, with which you will direct the misfortuned,[18] whose rigor you will dominate at your whim; but hide the light and science from the common men, from the wicked and unintelligent."

The rebellious angels, initiated into high magic and transmitting it to vulgar men through indiscreet women, were the cause that primitive civilization collapsed and that the representatives of Cain disputed the possession of the world, which possession only knew how to escape when the earth was flooded by the flood. The flood, then, represents the universal confusion into which human beings fall when they ignore the laws of nature.

High magic, the true key of the cabala, says that science is reserved for men who are masters of their passions. Indeed, chaste nature does not hand over the keys of the bridal chamber to adulterers.

---

17 Let the reader know that *exotericism* is what can be said, while *esotericism* is what it is necessary to hide. See the difference from an *s* to an *x*.

18 Translator's note: Or "unfortunate".

That is why there are and will exist for all centuries of centuries two classes of men: the free and the slaves.

Man is born a slave to his passions; but he is manumitted for intelligence. Between those who know how to achieve their freedom and those who do not, freedom is impossible.

Reason has to reign, to obey instincts.

Chapter I

Advice from Solomon to His Son Rehoboam and to Those Who Will Dedicate Themselves to Magic

JONAS SUFURINO says, that in the book there are Hebrew characters written on immaculate parchment; he was provided with the infernal spirits, with whom for most of his life he had dealings, in addition to Solomon's clavicle, containing the advice that this layman gave his son Roboan in his famous book, *The Secret of Secrets*,[19] so that said son, in turn, should bequeath it to all those human beings who will dedicate themselves to the study of magical sciences.

The translator of the *Sorcerer's Treasure*,[20] of which this is an appendix, having encountered great difficulties, not all of those writings were published in said book: but today the enlargement of the work has been entrusted to a person who for many years has been dedicated to this kind of study. We can offer our readers the advice of the wise king, which, even when addressed individually to his aforementioned son Roboan, can benefit our readers, and particularly those who, like the aforementioned king, always want to be free from iniquity, evil and impurity.

---

19 Translator's note: See Joseph Peterson, *True Black Magic: La Veritable Magie Noir*, Twilit Grotto Press, 2017; also Peterson, *Grimorium Verum*, CreateSpace Publishing, 2007. There are several excellent texts bearing this title, see also Michael-Albion MacDonald, *Secret of Secrets: The Unwritten Mysteries of Esoteric Qabbalah*, Heptangle Books, 1986.

20 Translator's note: A reference to *The Book of Saint Cyprian*, as discussed in the introduction.

Here now is the verbatim translation of those tips:

OF GOD'S LOVE

Divine love must proceed from the acquisition of the science that I profess, and the principle of this is the key to the fear of God. It is, therefore, necessary to honor him and adore him with true contrition and devotion, and to invoke him in all those things that we want to do or that we expect from him.

God, if he sees our requests are founded and the acts that we propose to carry out are just, he will lead us on the right path.[21]

When you want to learn the science of the magical arts it is necessary that you prepare and repair the order of lunations,[22] without which you will not be able to do anything useful; but if you observe them decently and sanely, together with the fear of God and virtue, which is what love of God consists of, you will be able to easily receive the achievement of your undertaking.

OF THE VIRTUE AND HOUR OF THE PLANETS

Of the tables of the hours and planets, you should have them present whenever you try to do something.

The hours between night and day are twenty-four, and each interval has a planet that dominates it, and since there are seven planets, divide those times between the twenty-four hours of the day and you will obtain the result that each planet dominates during the day, three hours, twenty-five minutes and forty-three seconds, in addition to the day of which dominion corresponds.

Bear in mind, therefore, that each planet dominates one day during the seven that each quarter moon has, in the way that is

---

21 Translator's note: At the end of this sentence is noted: "Si, no, no".
22 Translator's note: "lunaciones" or Lunar cycles.

indicated in the *Book of Saint Cyprian* (page 34), and that it also exercises dominion during a period of time on each day of the week.

It is very important to know the hours that each planet exerts its influence for magical operations; we give below a detailed review of them:

Saturn dominates from twelve at night until three thirty in the morning; *Jupiter* from three thirty to seven; *Mars* from seven to ten thirty; the *Sun* from ten thirty to two in the afternoon; *Venus* from two to five thirty; *Mercury* from half past five to eight, and the *Moon* from a quarter past eight to twelve at night.[23]

The hours of Saturn are good, like Mars in its days, in which it joins with the Moon to make experiments of hatred, judgments and discord. The hours of the Sun, Jupiter, and Venus, especially on the days when their dominance is complete,[24] are excellent to approve all the experiments, both ordinary and extraordinary, and those of Venus, especially in the day, of love. The Moon, being opposite the Sun and full of light, is good for experiments of war, noise and discord, and when it is in its last quarter, for experiments that tend to destroy or ruin. The Moon, when it is in its new quarter,[25] that is, when it does not receive the solar rays, or the last ones, is good for doing death experiments.

You must observe, inviolably, that when the Moon is in conjunction with the Sun you will not have started anything, because this time is very unfortunate and nothing should take place; but when the Moon fully receives the force of the Sun, you

---

23 Translator's note: Many of the classic grimoires list hours of the day that certain operations should be performed.

24 It is known in magic that even when a planet dominates the universe for one day, the moral dominance of another planet produces influences that can be, in all that they reach, harmful or beneficial.

25 Translator's note: "cuarto".

will be able to write, operate and prepare all the experiments you want to do, and mainly to speak with the spirits of the dead.

Regarding these experiments, I advise you to avoid them as much as possible, since the immortality of the soul being an essentially consoling dogma, all those who, due to earthly passions, vices or impure inclinations should fear a punishment, more or less bloody, try to disturb the peace and harmony that is due to those who have left their material covering on earth.

Besides—take a good look at this—the souls of the dead are around us. The beings whom we have loved in life can see us and even appear to us, but only by their gaze, that is, through the common mirror, which is light.

Chapter II

How Men Learned Magic

YOU MUST know, my son—continues Solomon in *The Secret of Secrets*—that magical science has not been transmitted to men in the way that Henoch describes in his famous book,[26] and whose form is the following:

In the first epoch of creation, there were angels from heaven who descended to earth to love women.

Because back then, when the daughters of men multiplied, young people of great beauty were born.[27]

And when the angels, the children of heaven, saw them, they fell in love with them.

And they said to each other:

— Let us descend to earth, choose our wives and beget children with them.

Then their chief, Samyasa,[28] told them:

— Perhaps you will not have the courage to fulfill that resolution, and I will then be the only one responsible for your fall.

And they replied:

— We swear that we will not repent, and carry out our wish.

---

26 Translator's note: There are also several versions of *The Book of Enoch*, notably translated by Richard Laurence, London, 1883; most recently by Wizards Bookshelf, 1973, 1976.

27 Translator's note: The Nephilim, biblical offspring of the "sons of God" and the "daughters of men".

28 Translator's note: A fallen angel, his name translates "infamous rebellion"; he was originally considered the most powerful angel in heaven but went on to rebel against God, and he is in the hierarchy of heaven as the leader of the Watchers.

And there were two hundred who went down to the mountain of Armon.[29]

And it is since then that mountain is called *Armon*, which means the mountain of the oath.

Those two hundred angels had their chiefs, Samyasa being the superior of all.

The names of the others are as follows: Urakabarameel, Azibeel, Tamiel, Ramuel, Danel, Azkeel, Sarakuyal, Asael, Armers, Batraal, Anane, Zabeve, Samraveel, Ertrael, Turel, Joniael, and Arazial.

And they took as wives the daughters of men, with whom they mixed and married, teaching them magic sciences, incantations, the value of roots and plants, and astrology.

Amazarac taught all the secrets of sorceries and enchantments; Barkaial was the teacher of astrologers; Akibeel revealed the signs of the cabala, and Azaradel the movement of the Moon and the influence it exerted on creation.

And God forgave them their rebellion in merit of their virtues and the love they always professed for him.

Their women were experts in the magical sciences, they revealed to other men the secrets they learned from their husbands, and magic was distributed throughout the world where the children of men lived.

The true tradition of the origin of true magic is the one that I am now going to refer to you:

You know very well, my son, that our father Adam had two sons, Cain and Abel. The first represented brutal force; the second the sweetness and lucidity of intelligence.

Both were not able to agree, and one of them had to disappear from the face of the earth. The rope broke on the

---

29 Translator's note: Mt. Hermon, deriving its name from the Hebrew word "herem", a curse.

weaker side.[30] Abel perished at the hands of his own brother, and thus the inheritance of the unfortunate Abel was passed, with profit, to a third son, named Seth.

And Seth, who was just, got everything from the Supreme Maker, from the Superior Spirit, even the entrance into paradise, whence his parents were thrown out, without the cherub who was on guard being able to prevent him with his withering sword.[31]

Seth represents, therefore, the primitive initiation.

And what did Seth see when he entered paradise? That the tree of science and the tree of life had joined to form one.

Do you know that he represents this fact? The agreement of religion with magic and high cabala.

When Seth left the paradise, the guardian cherub gave him three seeds of the trees *vitae et scienciae*,[32] which contained all the life force of them.

This fact represents the cabalistic ternary.[33]

When Adam died, Seth followed the instructions of the cherub, placed the three grains of seed in the mouth of his expiring father as a recompense or promise of eternal life.

The branches that sprouted from those three grains formed the burning brambles,[34] in the midst of which God revealed to Moses his eternal name. Here are those mysterious signs:[35]

---

30 Translator's note: "La cuerda se rompio por el lado mas debil".

31 Translator's note: "espada fulminante".

32 Translator's note: Of life and knowledge.

33 Translator's note: Trilogy or triad.

34 Translator's note: "zarzas encendidas".

35 Translator's note: The letters here are distorted, but appear to be Aleph Heh Yod Heh Aleph Teth (?) Yod Aleph Heh Yod (or Resh) Heh (the Hehs appear as either Cheh or Tau).

אחידאטיראתרה

The translation of them is as follows:

THE BEING THAT HAS BEEN, THE BEING THAT IS, AND THE BEING
THAT WILL BE.[36]

Moses, when God disappeared, took a triple bouquet of
those brambles and by divine inspiration he built his magic or
miraculous wand with them.

This rod, although separated from its trunk, did not cease to
live or flourish, being preserved in the ark. The rod that worked
so many wonders was replanted by my father, King David, on
Mount Zion, from which grew a mighty and gigantic tree, on
which the death of the Messiah was announced by prophets and
magicians.

I, in turn, knowing the mystery of the sacred tree, tried to
honor it in the human form, that I could make of its three trunks
the two symbolic columns of which it is spoken, in front of the
temple and to which, after they were covered with bronze, I put
the name of *Boaz* and *Jachin*.[37] They represented day and night,
vice and virtue, the angel and the devil. The remaining trunk
was ordered to be placed on the frontispiece of the main door of
the temple, as a talisman that would prevent any person who was
impure from entering it.

So far the Solomon tradition, which Saint Cyprian is in
charge of completing in the following way:

The Levites being corrupted, after the wise king died, they
uprooted the trunk during the night, which served as a barrier to

---

36 Translator's note: "El ser que ha sido, el ser que es y el ser que sera".

37 Translator's note: "Jakin y Bohas", the brass or bronze pillars in
front of Solomon's temple.

their iniquities, and threw it, after having loaded it with stones in order to prevent it from floating, into the probationary pool.[38]

From that moment on, a celestial spirit stirred the waters of the pool to communicate a miraculous virtue that had the object of inviting men to seek the tree of Solomon, that is true wisdom.

But the ignorance of the Jews, corrupted by vices, was supine, and they did not manage to understand what was the cause of the rising waters.

Only at the time when Jesus Christ was to enter Jerusalem, when cleaning the pool, did they find that immense log, useless according to them, for which they placed it in the guise of a pontoon across the Cedron stream.

And it was on that pontoon which Jesus Christ passed after his night arrest in the Orchard of the Olives;[39] and it was on that pontoon that his enemies pushed him to fall into the torrent,[40] and those who, in their haste to prepare, in advance, the instrument of torture,[41] took with them such a bridge, which was a three-section beam, formed by three different woods, and of which they made the cross on which a few days later they crucified the Redeemer of the world.

This allegory contains all the high traditions of the Cabala and the secrets only disclosed by Solomon and Saint John.

---

38 Translator's note: "la piscina probatica".

39 Translator's note: "Huerto de las Olivas".

40 Translator's note: "Torrente Cedron"; the text seems to allude to an extracanonical tradition similar to that reflected in Luisa Piccarreta, *The Hours of the Passion of Our Lord Jesus Christ*, hour nine: "O my Jesus, we are now at the Cedron Stream, and the wicked Jews shove you in. As they do this, they make you strike so hard against a rock there, that from your mouth you shed your most precious blood, leaving that rock marked with it."

41 Translator's note: "el instrumento del suplicio".

And, in this way, Seth, Moses, David, Solomon and Jesus took from the same cabalistic tree their scepters of kings or their rods of great Pontiffs.[42]

---

42 Translator's note: "Grandes Pontifices".

Chapter III

The Talismans[43]

KNOW, dear son Roboan, that the sacred name of JEHOVAH breaks down to seventy-two explanatory names, and whose whole is called the *Shem HaMephorash*.[44] The art of using these seventy-two names and finding the keys to universal science is what is called the *clavicle* in magic.

This *clavicle* is made up of *seventy-two* magic circles, and each two circles form a talisman. It turns out, then, that with these seventy-two names that *thirty-six* talismans are formed. It is four times *nine*, the *absolute number*, multiplied by the *quaternary*.[45] These talismans each bear two of the seventy-two names, with the emblematic sign of its name and that of the four letters of Jehovah's name, to which they correspond.

The Shem HaMephorash, or set of the seventy-two names of God, has served to form the so-called DIVINE TALISMAN, which is the one that in itself contains all the sacred letters with which the already mentioned seventy-two names are formed, and also some of the most principal names of the Supreme Creator. He has sovereign dominion over all spirits.

---

43 This chapter serves as a complement or extension to what was said in *The Book of Saint Cyprian*, for which we do not extend ourselves in greater detail.

44 Translator's note: "Shemhamphorash", the "hidden name" and/or the 72 names of God.

45 Translator's note: The names of God of four letters, most notably in Hebrew, Yod Heh Vau Heh.

Here is the drawing of it:[46]

Talismán divino

DIVINE TALISMAN

So far Solomon speaks—says Jonas Sufurino, the author of *The Book of Saint Cyprian,* having to add that of those talismans, thirty-five are consecrated to the seven planets, the great *dominatur* talisman being the one that makes the number thirty-six.

The knowledge, then, of the *clavicle* depends on the use and knowledge of talismans, which are very necessary in all acts of life, because they contain the ineffable and very holy names that were traced by the finger of God.

The talismans, once made according to the magical practices and wrapped in a silk cloth of art, will be consecrated in the following way: You will take a clay cup, in which you will place a

---

46 Translator's note: See page 115 of Stephen Skinner & David Rankine, *The Veritable Key of Solomon,* Golden Hoard Press, 2008, 2013. Note the talisman "for Sunday Under the Sun".

new lit charcoal, with male incense, or mast or olive wood; after
the exorcism and purification, you will trace with the *dagger of art*
on a virgin parchment the following circle:[47]

Círculo para la consagración de los talismanes

CIRCLE FOR THE CONSECRATION OF TALISMANS

You will take the talismans out of the cloth in which you
wrapped them before, and after perfuming with fragrant aromas,
you will enter the circle, and with your face turned to the east, you
will devoutly read the psalms: "Domine Dominus noster", "Caeli
enarrant gloriam Dei".[48] And it is said later: "Oh Adonay very
powerful! Alpha and Omega, who have made your people march

---

47 Translator's note: Around the outside of the talisman are the
directional words, Oriente, Septentrion, Occidente, Mediodia; inside
the ring of the talisman are Adonay, Accos, Jehova, Sabaoth; in the
middle of the talisman is the phrase Vas Terrena Magister.

48 Translator's note: "Our Lord God", and "The heavens declare the
glory of God"; these are Psalms 8 and 18, respectively.

over the sea on dry feet and who have accepted Abraham, your faithful servant, to the seed of which you have promised that all the tribes of the earth would be blessed, of which seed you have multiplied like the stars; that you have given Moses the law on Mount Sinai and that you have given to Solomon, your servant, the talismans for the safety of soul and body, with humility we beg you, O Majesty! that by your Power these talismans are consecrated, in order that they obtain virtue, and for the empire and principality they will be without end. Amen."

After this, you will perfume them again and keep them in the bag, always following the prescriptions established in *The Book of Saint Cyprian*, of which this is an appendix.

Chapter IV

Invocations, Evocations and Spells of Solomon.
Invocation to the Celestial Spirits

SOLOMON, according to the primitive *Book of Saint Cyprian*, only made evocations of the infernal spirits in those moments in which he wanted to torment[49] them, so that they would not tempt his subjects, but instead he was constantly in relationship with the celestial spirits, and especially in those cases in which he desired to enlighten his understanding.

Having established the hierarchy of said heavenly spirits in the primitive *Book of Saint Cyprian*, it only remains for us to expand it with some details, that is, the way in which he performed those invocations, after having placed the ring on the middle finger, in which only the name of the spirit whom he was trying to invoke would vary.

Here is that formula:

O Supreme Creator, most loving Father of all living beings, allow this one of your making, that the imponderable spirit of... (here one should indicate the name), appear to me, in order to encourage me in my enterprise or enlighten with its lights my limited and mortal intelligence!

Oh you ... (here the name of the invoked spirit), show yourself and help me in my prayers, and illuminate the intelligence of this humble servant of the Lord, forever and ever! Amen.[50]

---

49 Translator's note: "mortificarlos". Or "mortify".

50 Translator's note: See Skinner and Rankine, *Veritable Key of Solomon*.

In this same way, says Jonas Sufurino, all beings initiated into magic can invoke the celestial spirits in all those moments of life in which they need their protection.

However, it is necessary to bear in mind that the revelations or secrets have as their object divine, natural, or human things. Thus, there is an imperative need to ask for little and to choose well what is asked. It is also necessary to look first at the nature of the thing that is asked, and then ask God to grant grace, in the following way, indicated in the *Enchiridion Leonis Papae*:[51] In laudem et honorem Dei ac proximi utilitatem.[52]

EXORCISM TO FORCE THE DEMON TO RETURN A WRITTEN PACT

Clementissime Deus, cujus potentiae non est finis, qui in omnes creaturas tuas et res earum supremum habes semperque retines dominium, ita ut nihil sit quod tuo etiam per apostasiam eximi possit imperio; peccarimus in te, tuamque provocabimus justissimam iracundiam, quando tuis mandatis non obedibimus, atque tunc maxime quando ab amicitia tua et Domino fugientes, te abnegabinus et impiorum daemonorum consortio nos adjunximus; et cuasi non sufficeret abnegase te, etiam per scripturam nos daemonibus obligarimus et chiragraphim illud voluntarie obligationis contra te illi tradidimus asservandum. Verum clementissime Domine quia misericordiae quoque tuae

---

51 Translator's note: One of the earliest classical grimoires, the *Enchiridion of Pope Leo III*, Lyon, 1601. Also see Daniel Harms, James Clark and Joseph Peterson, *The Book of Oberon: A Sourcebook of Elizabethan Magic*, Llewelyn Publications, 2015. Also see Crossed Keys by Michael Cecchetelli, Scarlet Imprint, 2011, which includes an English translation of the *Enchiridion*.

52 Translator's note: Latin, "To the praise and honor of God and the good of our neighbor".

non est numerus, et tibi proprium est misereri semper et parcere; haec tua creatura, quae te abnegato se daemonibus tradito chirographo obligavit, in se infinita tua bonitate reversa, suam detestatur impretatem, et timore tuo compuncta, abnegato sursus daemone, tibi vero suo Domino subdi, atque in gratiam tuam recigri contrito corde desiderat. Scimus, Domine, te cor contritum et humiliatum nunquam despicere, neque chirographum illud misericordiae tuae ullum impedimentum ponere posse, ideoque supptices te deprecamur, ub abundantia pietatis tuae non tantum hujus peccati impieratem per Sanguinem Filii tui Domini nostri Jesu Christi remittas, sed et daemonum ad restituendum chirographum obligationis et traditionis illius verbo virtutis luce compellas; ne de sua tyrannide glorietur, ne jus aliquod praetendat in hominen, quem per Filium tuum peccatorum suorum vinculis absolvi deprecamur. Per eumdem Dominum nostrum Jesum Christum Filium tuum. Amen.[53]

After having read this exorcism with true contrition and fervor, the supplicant will spit three times in front of him, and the pact will be ipso facto completely null and void, even though when turning his back, the supplicant will not find behind him the pact he signed, because Satan was forced by the spell to return the signed document.

---

53 Translator's note: See Appendix for an English translation of the Latin prayer.

Chapter V

The Secret of the Sphinxes

La esfinge

THE SPHINX

WHAT MY predecessors—writes Solomon in his aforementioned book—, called the four elements (air, fire, earth and water), are not for magic more than four elemental forms of the single substance.

These forms were represented by the sphinx, in the following way: the air, by the wings; the water, by the woman's bosom; the earth, by the body of the bull, and the fire, by the claws of the lion.

Substance is one, three times triple, as an essence, and, finally, quadruple in the form of existence. Such is the secret of the three pyramids, triangular in elevation, square at the base and guarded by sphinxes.

Egypt, in raising these monuments, had wanted to place the herculean columns[54] of universal science.[55]

The shape of the sphinxes also represents, by hieroglyphic analogy, the four properties of the universal magic agent:[56] dissolve, coagulate, heat, cool.

These four properties, directed by the will of man, can modify all forms of nature and produce, according to the impulse given, life or death, health or disease, love or hate, wealth or poverty. Finally, they can place all the reflections of light at the service of the imagination, since they are the natural solution to the most daring and most concrete questions that future generations could address to high magic.

These questions and answers can be condensed into the form that you will see below.

---

54 Translator's note: "columnas de Hércules".

55 The sands of the arid desert in which these pyramids today rise, will undoubtedly have changed their place, just as the centuries have passed; but they are always mighty and majestic, they propose to the nations an enigma, whose word have been lost. As for the sphinx, it seems to have darkened more and more, under the dust of the ages. The great empires of Daniel have reigned turn by turn over the earth, and they have collapsed under their own weight into the tomb of non-being. Conquests of war, foundations of work, works of human passions, all have been swallowed up by the symbolic body of the sphinx. However, the human head alone rises above the desert sands, as if waiting for the day when the universal empire of thought must be consolidated.

Translator's note: "tumba del no ser".

56 Today we would call it light or astral fire.

Translator's note: "agente magico universal".

Chapter VI

The Paradoxical Questions to the Sphinxes and Their Answer

THE QUESTIONS

The paradoxical questions that human curiosity, in its crazy or vain recklessness, can ask, must be considered eightfold, and they are the following:

1. Can you escape death?
2. Does the philosopher's stone exist? If it exists, what to do to find it?
3. Can the terrestrial being be served by the spirits?
4. What are my clavicle, my scepter and my ring?
5. Can the future be foreseen by true calculations?
6. Can good or evil be done by magical influences?
7. What do you have to do to be a true magician?
8. What do the forces of true black magic and Red Magic consist of?

THE ANSWERS

Q. – *Can you escape death?*
A. – In two ways: In *time*, curing and preventing diseases: in *space*, perpetuating personal identity in the transformations of existence through memory.

Life is the result and cannot be preserved except by the succession and perfection of forms. The science of perpetual or continuous motion is that of life and that of nature. This science, which has been revealed to me by otherworldly spirits, has for its object the just weight of balanced influences.

You must bear in mind, therefore, that all renewal is operated by destruction, and that thus all generation is death and all death a generation.

Q. – *Does the philosopher's stone exist? If it does, what to do to find it?*

A. – Metals in the bowels of the earth are formed like planets in space, due to the specialties of a latent law that decomposes them, crossing different environments.

To seize a medium in which the metallic light is latent before it specializes and place it at the extreme and positive pole, that is to say red-hot, obtained by chance or borrowed by the light itself, such is the whole secret of the *great work*. It is understood that this positive light, in its extreme degree of condensation, is life itself made fixed and can serve as a universal solvent and medicine for all kingdoms of nature.

But, to remove the mask,[57] the *wheat*,[58] the arsenic, its metallic, live and androgynous sperm, first a solvent is necessary, which can be a saline mineral monster, but rely upon the help of electricity and magnetism.[59]

The rest is done by itself, in a single glass, in a single stove and by the graduated fire of a single lamp.

Q. – *Can the terrestrial being be served by the spirits?*

A. – The spirits only put themselves at the service of sovereign beings who know how to chain their turbulence, order their appetites and restrain their passions.

The immortality of the soul is a consoling dogma and those who have the recklessness to look towards the afterlife with the

---

57 Translator's note: "mascarita".

58 Translator's note: "aestibium".

59 Translator's note: One example of evidence that this text is not drawn from medieval texts or earlier, as the scientific topics of electricity and magnetism are not really known during that time, other than such basic matters as lightning and the compass.

eyes of earthly existence must fear punishment. That is why the evoked dead appear with sad and angry eyes, and complaining of having disturbed them in their repose, they only utter complaints and threats.

Q. – *What are my clavicle, my scepter and my ring?*

A. – My keys or clavicles are rational and religious forces manifested by signs, and which serve less for evocations than to preserve men from committing aberrations in experiences related to magic.

The *seal* summarizes the *keys*; the ring indicates the use.

My ring is both square and circular, representing the mystery of squaring the circle.

It is made up of seven squares, arranged to form a circle. Two settings are adapted to it, one circular, made of gold, and the other, square, made of silver.

The hoop must be made of filigree of seven metals.

In the silver setting a white stone is set, and in the gold one red, with these signatures:

On the white, the sign of the *macrocosm*.

On the red is the sign of the *microcosm*.

When the ring is placed on the finger, one of the stones must face outwards and the other inwards, depending on whether you want to send the spirits of light or the powers of darkness.

I will explain the power of this ring.

The will is all powerful when armed with the forces of nature.

The thought is dead or idle, as long as it is not manifested by the verb or by the sign, it not being able then to excite or direct the will.

The sign is the necessary form of thought and the indispensable instrument of the will.

The more perfect the sign, the stronger is the formula of thought, and consequently, the more powerful the force of the will.

If blind faith transports mountains, what will a faith enlightened by a complete and immutable science not do?

My ring, with its double seal, is all the science and faith of the magicians, summed up in one sign. It is the symbol of all the forces of heaven and earth and of the holy laws that govern them, whether in the celestial macrocosm or in the human microcosm.

It is the talisman of talismans and the pentacle of magic.

Q. – *Can the future be foreseen by certain calculations?*

R. – Nothing in life happens by chance. Chance is the unforeseen, but the unforeseen by the ignorant has been foreseen by the wise.

Every event, like every form, results from a conflict or a balance of forces, and these forces can be represented by numbers.

The future can be determined by calculation. All violent action is determined by calculation.

The future is in the past and the past is in the future. When the genius foresees, he remembers. Effects are so necessarily and exactly linked to causes that, in turn, they become new causes of effect, so conforming to the former in their way of production, that a single fact can reveal to the seer a whole genealogy of mysteries.

Furthermore, Moses has said: "The law of the Lord is written on your forehead and on your hands."[60]

Q. – *Can good or evil be done by magical influence?*

A. – The will of man modifies everything, to the point that the sole impulse of a man can change the balance of a world. The smallest of these could in one breath, expanding the latent

---

60 See the mysteries of the hand and the countenance.

———

Translator's note: Exodus 13:9 – "This observance will be for you like a sign on your hand and a reminder on your forehead that this law of the Lord is to be on your lips".

heat of our earth, make it explode and disappear into space like a small cloud of ash. How much, then, would it take for him with another breath to vanish the happiness of his fellow men?

Men are magnetized like the worlds, and they radiate their special light like the sun. Some are absorbent, the other irradiators. No one is isolated in the world: every man is a fatality or a providence.

Q. – *What do you have to do to be a true magician?*

A. – The man who possesses the hidden forces of nature, without exposing himself to being crushed by them, is a true magician.

It will be recognized in his works and in his end, that he is always a continual sacrifice.

Q. – *What are the forces of true magic?*

A. – In seeking balance, which is order and movement, that which is science. The science of balance and movement is the absolute science of nature.

Man, through this science, can produce and direct natural phenomena, always rising to a higher and more perfect intelligence than his own. Magic can be said, therefore, to be the means used by the exalted divinity for men to reach the supreme perfection.

Part Two

ALCHEMY

COOKBOOK OF THE TRUE MAGICIAN

Chapter I

Secret to Obtain a Perpetual Youth

YOU WILL go every five decades (twenty-five years),[61] on a trip to the countryside, as a jubilee, that will last just forty days, taking care that it begins during the full moon of the month of May, accompanied by a person who is very devoted[62] to you and very faithful, and to whom you will not reveal your purposes in any way.

You will ensure that the house in which you are to stay has clean and ventilated conditions, and above all—this is the most essential part—that it is close to fields where white wheat has been sown. After you have made the preparations that will be indicated later, you will move to the chosen point and faithfully observe the following prescriptions:

You shall not drink any other liquid, except for those to be indicated, than the May dew, collected on the green wheat fields at dawn on a pure, new white linen cloth, nor shall you eat anything other than fresh and tender herbs.

---

61 Translator's note: "Haras cada cinco lustros (veinticinco anos)...".

62 Translator's note: "adicta".

You will begin the brief snacks with a large cup of said dew and you will finish them with a cake or a simple crust of bread, taking care not to fill the stomach, nor with many of the indicated herbs, nor with too many crusts of bread.

Fasting is the key to the operation, therefore, only what is strictly necessary should be ingested to sustain forces and moisten the digestive vessels.

You can, however, drink the dew water already indicated for all herbs.

On the seventeenth day you will perform a slight bloodletting upon yourself if possible.

From that day on, and after the small bleeding, you will take six drops of azoe balsam[63] every morning, increasing the dose daily by two drops until you reach the thirty-second day, in which you will renew the small emission of blood in the morning twilight hour, immediately lying down on the bed, from which you will not get up until the end of the quarantine.

After the first bleeding, you will take, on awakening, a first grain of *universal medicine*, that is, a compound of *astral mercury combined with golden sulfur*.[64]

You will then feel a swoon that must last six consecutive days with their corresponding nights; later convulsions, perspiration and considerable evacuations.

You will then change your underwear and bedding.

When the evacuations have concluded, you will take a broth having been made or simmered, seasoned with rue leaves, sage, valerian, verbena and lemon balm.

The next day, you will have a second grain of *universal medicine*, and the next day a warm bath.

---

63 Translator's note: From the Zoe Balsam plant.

64 The composition of both things are expressed in the course of this treatise.

On the thirty-sixth day (day 36), you will drink a glass of Egyptian wine.

At the thirty-seventh, you will take the third and last grain of *universal medicine*.

A deep sleep will follow.

The hair, teeth, nails and skin will be renewed, wrinkles, if you have them, disappearing from the face.

On the thirty-eighth day you will take a warm bath with the aromatic herbs mentioned above.

On the thirty-ninth day you will pour and take in two tablespoons of red wine, ten drops of the elixir of Acharab.[65]

At the fortieth (40) and last, the work will be finished and the decrepit will be rejuvenated.

Then you will try to prepare the stomach to take and endure the foods you were used to before.

---

65 Translator's note: One name for "the elixir of life", also known as "elixir of immortality" and sometimes equated with the "philosopher's stone", a potion that supposedly grants the drinker eternal life and/or eternal youth. This elixir was also said to cure all diseases.

Chapter II

Glorious Water for the Preparation of Potable Gold

HERMES TRISMEGISTUS says in his *Emerald Tablet*,[66] not enigmatically, that *quod est superius est sicut a quod est inferius*, etc.,…[67] proving that it must be understood that the heavens and elements are essentially and substantially the same thing, and are only accidentally distinguished by the heavens being incorruptible and the elements participating in corruption.

The philosopher, ignoring that in natural things there are other principles, or anything other than the elements, without resolution doubts how some principles can be corruptible and others incorruptible.

As of the corruptible elements, they can be made incorruptible, which is what the vulgar doubt, and even many educated men, albeit inexperienced in the magical arts, since those initiated in them hid them under indecipherable enigmas, this being what I am going to explain, telling you that where in magic or in the sacred books you will read of *mana or nectar*, you should understand that it is the *elixir of life, the universal remedy, the potable gold*.

---

66 Translator's note: "Tabla de Esmeralda".

67 Translator's note: "That which is above is like that which is below".

How, then, is this medicine manufactured, with which Cledea reduced Janson to youth,[68] and with which Aesculapius raised the almost dead?[69]

One takes crude mercury, as it comes out of the mines, two pounds; by washing it with strong vinegar and common salt, make it clear and sparkling like a mirror. Once this operation is done, you wipe it with a cloth or a sponge, in order to remove all the moisture it may have from the vinegar. Then take four pounds of *Roman vitriol*,[70] which you will dry in the sun or over a gentle fire, slowly, until it becomes white ash.

Then take a pound of said mercury, two of the aforementioned vitriol, one of common salt twice dissolved, washed and frozen, and grind the whole on clean stone until the mercury is completely mixed between the ashes of the vitriol and the salt.

Then place this amalgam in a long-necked glass vial, and put it in a pan filled with ash or sand, starting the soft fire until all the moisture has come out of the materials, then increasing the fire little by little and gradually. When the mercury has risen to the sides of the glass, white as snow and shining like glass, you let it cool, break and remove the sublimated mercury, being able to observe that when removing the excretion from the mercury, it has the same primitive weight because of having taken from the vitriol sulfide that which was lost in excretion.

Take again a pound and a half of the same vitriol and eight ounces of salt and grind it with the sublimated, and when these ingredients are well mixed, you will put them to sublimate in the same way as before. This sublimation will be repeated seven times, always adding salt and new Roman vitriol, throwing away

---

68 Translator's note: "Cledea redujo a Janson a la juventud".

69 Translator's note: "Esculapio resucitaba a los casi muertos." Asclepius is the Greek god of healing and medicine, and the son of Apollo.

70 Translator's note: Copper sulfate.

the excretion on each occasion you carry out the operation until the pure and sublimated mercury remains, which will be known in that, clear as crystal and white as snow, it will be flexible like wax. But be warned that in any glass you do not put more than one pound of mercury so that it can be prepared very well, taking the necessary amount from the preparation.

And you will know how, having done this, you will prepare the *philosophical lunary* herb,[71] of which all the sages have dealt in their books, extracting from it the red wine called *lunary liquor*, extracted in the following way:

Take two pounds of said *lunary* and put it in a luted glass, which should not be very large, taking care that two-thirds of it remain empty; close the top of the retort[72] well, as well as all its joints, and place it in the alchemists' stove. After it is dried, cover the top above so that the flame will reverberate in time. You will at the beginning make gentle fire and thus little by little you will increase it until you see a certain red water falls from the retort to the container, dense like liquid honey. Then continue to fan the fire while you see that it distills, and when it does not distill more, increase the fire so that all the liquor comes out. When, no matter how big the fire, nothing comes out, let it cool for three days, so that the mercury spirits settle in the container, because they are harmful. Then remove the luting[73] from the joints and open the glasses and the same container, without removing the matter, having removed the retort from the stove, you will join another

---

71 Translator's note: Willow.

72 Translator's note: A device used for distillation or dry distillation of substances. It consists of a spherical vessel with a long downward-pointing neck.

73 Translator's note: Conjectural reading of "el luto".

retort with another two pounds of the *lunaria*[74] that you will distill again as before, continuing in the same way until the liquor has been extracted from all the lunaria, which will be conserved to make a divine *brandy*.[75]

And when you reach this point, you should know that the liquor you have extracted is the same one that the wise men obscurely treat, that is, the blond wine,[76] which Aristoteles and Raimundo Lulio[77] called *nigrum, nigrius, nigro*.

All the excretions that remain, after having removed the liquor, you will throw them to the waste site, because they are of no value, like damaged and useless earth, of mercury and Roman vitriol.

Learn now to extract a spirit from your wine.

Put a pound of the said liquor or red wine, as you want to call it, in a glass vessel, not very wide, and with its alembic and container very well closed at the joints, so that in no way can it breathe, and put it in a water bath on the athanor.[78] You will give fire to the bath so sweet and gentle that you can have your hand in it without burning yourself, and with the said gentle heat it will come out and distill a clear water like common water. Therefore, let all the water distill, which will come out of your wine in four calendar days. Note that it is better to remove this water little by little with gentle heat, so that the air does not come out with it; because this celestial water is the quintessence of

---

74 Translator's note: Lunaria is from the Silver Dollar Plant, but this probably refers to the lunary herb discussed above.

75 Translator's note: "aguardiente divino".

76 Translator's note: "vino rubio".

77 Translator's note: Raymond Lull, who is spoken of as the first and greatest missionary who has ever gone to the Muslim world.

78 Translator's note: A furnace used to provide a uniform and constant heat for alchemical digestion.

mercury and the purest and most incorruptible part of it, which the alchemists looked for with special care. With all this, it has with it a superfluous and useless part, which received the name of *phlegm*, and which must be separated using the means that I will now describe, bearing in mind that this Benedict water[79] is extracted with moderate and gentle fire, so that twenty minutes intervenes between one drop and the next, and thus you will not err; and although I have told you that in four calendar days all the water will come out, even so, do not remove your wine from the water bath until you see that it does not expel any more water or steam.

Then let it cool, and remove the container. Cover it very well, so that your brandy does not evaporate.

The rectification of the spirit will be done in the following way: Take the water that you got from your red wine, and pour it in a glass flask, with its alembic[80] and container, the joints tightly closed. Put it in the aforementioned water bath, and through it you will distill your spirit again until not a single drop distills, and keep aside what remains in the flask, and return again to rectify your mercurial water in the same way until there are no more dregs in the flask, which will happen the fifth time; and although some alchemists have rectified it until the seventh, it can happen to be quite enough even in the fourth, as it remains without flame, which will be manifest to you if you burn a silver sheet and it is dissolved when it is put into it; because then it will be vinegar of the alchemists, soluble. With this water thus rectified, you will remove the spirit from the earth in this way:

---

79 Translator's note: Benedict's solution consists of copper sulfate pentahydrate, sodium carbonate, sodium citrate and distilled water.

80 Translator's note: A distilling apparatus, now obsolete, consisting of a rounded, necked flask and a cap with a long beak for condensing and conveying liquid to a container.

Distill all the liquor that is left as a naval fish,[81] liquify it, and then put it in the glass flask and pour it over the rectified liquor, in an amount that exceeds the matter by four fingers. Close your glass well, so that in no way can it breathe, and put it in a hot bath or in warm manure for six days, after which you extract your vial from there and put it in pans of sand or ashes, and, by alembic, remove all the mercurial water in which is infused the spirit that it carries with it, and keep it well covered apart. Then pour another quantity of the said mercurial water on the remaining dregs and put it in the said bath for another six days, in which time your matter will be digested and putrefied.

Then put the glass, being first cold, in sand or ashes, and extract the water, as you did before, for seven times, at the end of which you will have taken with it the spirit that was in its earth. Save this water; because it is animated water of which the wise men write so wonderfully and secretly, calling it by various names.

When you have removed all the spirit from the earth with the mercury water, as I taught you before, increase your fire little by little, and, distilling so, an oil will come out, much sought after by alchemists for various operations, and which they give different names.

Raimundo Lulio and Teophrasto[82] called this water vegetable brandy, a heavenly and fifth essence; therefore, if you want to reduce this water to incorruptibility, to turn from bitter and smelly to sweet and odorous, above all the fragrance of this world, in such a way that, after its digestion and maturity, only a drop can be drunk, which will remove all the diseases of the human body in the blink of an eye, and, by tempering other qualities, reduce them to equalization, and make those very close

81 Translator's note: "de pez naval".

82 Translator's note: Theophrastus, a Greek native of Eresos in Lesbos, was the successor to Aristotle in the Peripatetic school.

to death to live again, returning from old to young, you will work in the following manner:

Take the amount of this brandy you want, but at least three or four pounds, and put it in a glass, which is called circulatory; and if you do not have this glass, then in a goblet that has a long neck, and close it with another goblet, so that the mouth of the one that is empty enters the one that contains the mercurial water, and the joints of the double mouth are tightly closed, then place it in the athanor, and give it such heat that your hand can hardly support it, leaving the bowls in the fire for fifty or sixty calendar days, in which time your water will rise and fall, and, digesting itself, it will become sweet, or, at least, palatable.

After the time indicated, that is, fifty or sixty calendar days, look at your water and you will find it divided into two different parts; because the first part of the water that is above will be clear and resplendent like the sky, being our quintessence. On the other hand, the one that is below will be cloudy; for this reason, you will extract each one of them separately, keeping the clear part hermetically closed, so that it does not volatilize, which would happen if it found a way out, because it is very subtle, pure, diaphanous and volatile.

With this water you can always lengthen your life and make all diseases disappear from your body, also being the same one that brings metals to perfection; and although it is digestible and sweet, even so, it dissolves the metals of its own nature and makes them stronger. With this water, *potable gold* is also made, which is the *universal remedy*, in the way that you will see in the following chapter:

POTABLE GOLD

Take gold, well purified by grinding,[83] and scorching[84] according to art, in the quantity that suits you, mixing it with the same amount of the *glorious water*, in the previous chapter indicated, and close the mixture in the retort, so that it does not suffer the contact of the air. Once this operation is done, place this retort in a pan full of hot ashes, letting it remain there for one day with its corresponding night, giving it as much fire as it needs to boil gently, but continuously, and once one has passed as I have indicated, extract the vial from the ashes and put it in the bain-marie[85], letting the liquor digest for two days and nights, then putting to cool, set aside by a gentle inclination, that which is to be dissolved in a vessel, which you cover immediately, and place in another bath that is warm; because you must be sure that the dissolved water never gets cold. Then weigh the remaining matter, that is, the gold that is not dissolved, and pour over the other quantity an equal weight of your circulated menstrum,[86] and proceed as before, next emptying the solution into the first, and so you will continue in successive operations until all the gold is dissolved in the glorious water. And when your gold is all dissolved, put the total solution in a glass vial, and, placing it in a light bath, distill all the circulated mercurial water until in the bottom of the vial remains only a residue similar to soft wax. Place this matter in a cold and humid place, and in six calendar days everything will dissolve in clear water like a shining star. This water is *potable gold* and without corrosibility, raised with water of its own nature without mixture of strange things, of which *potable*

---

83 Translator's note: "cemento".

84 Translator's note: "calcinado".

85 Translator's note: A metal cup with handle.

86 Translator's note: "menstruo circulado", a solvent.

gold, if you only give a drop to a sick person, apparently dead, it will make him revive with the grace of God, turning him from an old man to a youth; but always taking into account:

Deus super omnia (God above all).

Chapter III

Magic Unions

EVERYONE initiated in black magic—says Jonas Sufurino—, must, before doing any experiment, and after the ritual ablutions,[87] rub the body with the *magic ointment,* doing the same with the people or neophytes who want to start in this science.

The magic anointing recommended by Saint Cyprian, and of which I have made use, is done in the following way:

Fresh butter .... 4 ounces.
Sage .... 4 adarmes.[88]
Rosemary .... 4 "
Verbena .... 4 "
Parsley .... 4 "
Belladonna root .... 2 "
Opium ....1 grain.

After crushing the aromatic plants well with the belladonna and opium, add their juice to the butter and beat well.

This ointment can be perfumed with essence of rose, geranium, violet, etc., etc.

---

87 Translator's note: A ritual bathing of the body.

88 Translator's note: The *adarme,* an antiquated Spanish unit of mass, equal to three *tomines,* each equivalent to 1 / 16 ounce, or 1.8 grams.

The ointment to prepare to attend the coven is made up of *condor fat*,[89] in which three grains of *astral mercury* and two of *asufre aureo*[90] are mixed.[91]

TO CURE JAUNDICE

Get yourself a good supply of earthworms and cook them in a new clay pot. When the cooking has been verified, strain the remaining water and add a quantity of honey, enough to sweeten the water and remove the bad taste. Of this concoction, you will drink two glasses a day, and before the week is through you will have been cured completely.

TO OBTAIN A WOMAN'S FAVORS

Take an apple that is very healthy and very beautiful, on a Friday before sunrise. Divide it into two pieces, and after having taken out the core and the seeds, put in their place a square piece of paper, on which you will have written, with your own blood, your name and surname and those of the person whose favors you wish to obtain. Then you put a second piece of paper that only contains the word *Scheva*[92] written in clear and legible characters. Once this operation is done, you will reunite the two papers and tie them with three hairs of the coveted person and another three of yours. Then you reunite the two pieces of the apple, by means

---

89 Translator's note: "manteca de condor".

90 Translator's note: A specific organic sulfur.

91 The *astral mercury* referred to here is nothing other than the *glorious water* that is described in the previous chapter; with regard to hard sulfur, in the course of this treatise the formula to obtain it will be explained.

92 Translator's note: See Appendix.

of two imperceptible pins made with green myrtle wood, having done which you will make it roast in the oven, wrap it in bay leaves and place it, finally, at the head of the bed in which the coveted person sleeps, without her noticing, and be sure that in a short time you will get her favors.

TO AVOID THE EVIL EYE

You can avoid it by enclosing in the quill of a male goose feather the Gospel of Saint John that begins, *In principium erat verbum*,[93] written on virgin parchment, with the ritual pen and ink, and wearing it hanging from a red silk cord around the neck.[94]

You will find this Gospel in The Enchiridion.

TO CURE EPILEPSY[95]

You will have a young silversmith make, when the moon is in its fullness, a very pure silver ring, destined to be worn on the middle finger of the left hand. In the setting of this ring you will place a piece of deer foot.

Once the ring is manufactured and when the moon is still in its fullness, or in conjunction with Jupiter or Venus, and at the favorable time of this planet, you will engrave by yourself, with the tip of the ritual lancet, the following inscription:

✠ Dabi ✠ Habi ✠ Habet ✠ Habi.

---

93 Translator's note: Latin, "In the beginning was the word".

94 In the fortuitous event of not carrying what has just been indicated, when perceiving the danger hide the thumb of the left hand between the palm of the hand and the other fingers.

95 Translator's note: "El mal caduco".

TO REMOVE THE POWER OF A MAN

You will take a firefly in summer, crush it in your hand and rub the nape of the person you want to make impotent with it, applying all your five senses in this task and mentally begging the infernal spirits to come and help you.

TO SATISFY SENSUAL DESIRES

You will carry on your chest, inside a bag made with wolf skin, the heart of a turtledove, and it is proven that the loving desires will be appeased in you, while you carry it on your person.

TO INFUSE COURAGE TO THE MOST COWARDLY MAN

You will try to supply yourself with lion bones and droppings, all of which you will grind perfectly in a new mortar. Once this operation has been carried out, you will pour the resulting powders into a bottle of white wine, adding to all this, in the proper proportion, sandalwood or mint leaves, nutmeg scraps and two or three branches of wormwood. After an infusion that will last a whole lunar cycle,[96] two glasses will be drunk a day, it being proven that at ten drinks, the fainthearted man becomes a true man of courage and energy.

TO DOMINATE PEOPLE

You will procure a snake of any species whatsoever. When this operation is carried out, you will enclose it in a large cage of metal mesh, feeding it small birds, which you will throw alive inside the cage, noticing well how it fascinates and attracts them

96 Translator's note: "novilunio".

and then devours them, and being careful, after having invoked to the spirits that are most conducive to you, to say mentally while the serpent executes the fascination, the following words: *This is how I want to dominate and attract people.*

Once this operation has been carried out for a week, you will cut off the head of the snake, which head you will keep in a bottle containing alcohol or ether, always trying to keep the aforementioned head in view. Then you will put the rest of the trunk of the mentioned reptile to dessicate in the sun, in its favorable hour. When it is well dessicated, you will infuse it with a good amount of excellent wine for seven days, after which you will begin to drink that wine, taking care to do so by looking at the head of the snake and saying: *Oh great spirit! Oh mighty Adonay! Make the attractive powers of that filthy reptile to pass to this your submissive servant, for the glory and benefit of creation.* Amen.

Once the previous operation has been carried out, the applicant will be invested with the *Dominatur* talisman, so that success is more immediate.

It is certain that whoever practices to the letter what is indicated here, he will be able to attract and dominate his peers, and that his gazes will attain an irresistible fascinating power.

FOR A BARREN WOMAN TO BECOME FERTILE

It is perfectly proven that the plant called *Latraea-clandestina*[97] is endowed with a magical virtue to make a woman fertile when for her entire life she has been sterile.

---

97 Translator's note: The purple toothwort, also known as "Clandestine", a parasitic plant species in the flowering plant family Orobanchaceae, native to western Europe.

To obtain this result, it is enough for the infertile woman to boil said plant, and when the cooking has been verified, put it in a kettle and sit on it in order to receive the vapor.

TO DRIVE A PERSON MAD

You will take crocodile egg shells, which you shall put into infusion, after you have crushed them very well, adding verbena, rue, marjoram and wormwood, in good Cyprus wine, for seven moons, after which you will filter the resulting liquor, giving it to drink to the person you want to drive crazy.

TO PUT DOWN A PERSON WITHOUT CAUSING ANY HARM

You will infuse six flowers of the solanifera plant called *papaver*[98] in rose liqueur for a quarter of the moon, after which time you will filter the liquor and give it to the person you want to lull.

TO MAKE A PERSON'S HAIR FALL OUT

You will take the left thigh of an ostrich, male or female, and fry it in peanut oil, with which you will rub the head of the person you want to see bald, being proven that the hair will never grow again.

TO HANDLE A RED-HOT IRON

Grind *carmine* augmented with rock *alum*, to which you will add *evergreen* juice and *laurel* residues in just proportions. The

---

98 Poppy.

person who rubs himself with that mixture could handle an iron made red-hot with impunity.

TO SEE IN A DREAM WHAT WILL HAPPEN TO THE PERSON WHO DOES THE EXPERIMENT

You will take curdled blood from an ass and mix it with tallow[99] from the chest of a lynx,[100] ensuring that equal parts enter the mixture. When the mixture is well compact, you will make balls of the size of a chickpea, which you will burn in your house when you give yourself to rest. When you sleep, a vision will appear to you during your dream and will instruct you in everything that should happen to you.

TO LIVE A LONG TIME WITHOUT EATING

You will take earth that has been purified by the rays of the sun inside a round glass vial and you will apply it on the navel, renewing it when it is too dry. With this you will be able to spend a long time without having to take any food.[101]

---

99 Translator's note: A fatty substance made from rendered animal fat, used in making candles and soap.

100 Translator's note: "lobo cerval"; from the Latin "lupus cervarius", referring to the Iberian lynx.

101 The divine Paracelsus has verified this experiment, as manifested in his works.

TO MAKE OBJECTS INCOMBUSTIBLE

Take fish *liga*[102] and mix it with an equal amount of alum, after which you will pour the mixture into wine vinegar. Varnish with this composition all the objects you want, which will become fireproof, at least as long as time has not destroyed the effects of the varnish.

TO MAKE THE UNIVERSAL ELIXIR

Choose a good red wine, thick, strong and well aged, to which you will add, in regular proportion, quicklime, well-pulverized brimstone, tartar made with good wine, and common salt, white and granulated; place all this in a well covered flask, next to which there will be an alembic, in which you will practice the distillation. This being produced, you will drink a glass of this elixir on an empty stomach, and not only will you be free of diseases, but you will feel fortified and rejuvenated.

TO MANUFACTURE 'WATER OF THE SUN'[103] WITH WHICH HONORS AND RICHES ARE OBTAINED

You will take a pot of fired clay, but not glazed, and you will put in it *sulfur of gold* and *astral mercury*. Once this is done, you will fill it with water and expose it every day to the rays of the sun during the hours that this planet dominates in the sky, after which you will remove the container to a damp and dark room, until the planet returns to dominate the environment again, repeating this operation until the liquid in the vessel has been absorbed by the solar rays. Then, in a new mortar, you will reduce such a vessel to

---

102 Translator's note: "liga de pescado"; maybe "garter", probably meaning "fish guts".

103 Translator's note:"agua de sol".

powder, which powder you will put into a flask that you will place in a room where no brightness penetrates, filling it afterwards with water from the river taken at sunrise.

This water, from which you will drink from now on, has great virtue, and if you drink with recollection and faith every morning at sunrise, at the same time that you invoke its protection, it will bring you honor and riches.

MAGIC CANDLE

If you know or have dreamed that there is a hidden treasure in a certain place, to find it it will be necessary that you make a thick *human tallow* candle, placing it in a hole that you will make in the center of a piece of hazelnut wood, cut in the shape of a horseshoe.

Lit in the underground where you are looking for the treasure, the flame will indicate to you by its oscillation and crackling that you are approaching it, extinguishing when you are on top of the object of your yearnings.

ROOSTER QUALITIES

A mysterious and cabalistic bird. Entirely white or black, it is used for all sorts of enchantments. His song puts to flight the demons that listen to him.

Of all the animals, he is the only male that, without any female, secretly lays a little egg, from which, in three just moons, a small snake whose gaze is deadly comes out.

VIRTUES OF THE LAUREL

The dry laurel has the virtue of predicting to those who question it, if an event will be successful or adverse. The omen will be dire if a laurel branch thrown into the fire burns. Conversely, the omen will be favorable if it burns with a loud crackling.

LICHNOMANCIA

When you want to guess what will befall you or what happens to you, buy three green candles and place them in as many candlesticks, which you will place on a triangle-shaped candelabrum. Once this is done, you will light them by means of a flammable object that does not bear sulfur, invoking at the same time the six main heads of the *salamanders*, which are: *Vehniah, Achajah, Jesabel, Jeliel, Cathethel* and *Mehahel*. Once the candles are lit, you will refrain from removing the wick, observing the accidents of the flame. You will deduce the oracles in the following way.

If the flame swings from left to right, an extraordinary event, good or bad.

If it spirals, intrigues from our enemies.

If it extinguishes, betrayal.

If it increases its radiance when blown upon, happiness and fortune.

Part Three

CHALDEAN AND EGYPTIAN MAGIC

Philters, Enchantments, Spells And Charms

Chapter I

Charms, Produced by the Virtues and Qualities of Toads[104]

It is very easy to perform this kind of spell, being, according to Saint Cyprian, the one that has the greatest power over all.

In the book of his history as a sorcerer, he says that the toad has a great invincible magical force, because the devil made a pact with it, since it is the food that Lucifer gives to the souls that are in hell.

For this reason, the charms and spells that we express below can be made with the toad.

SPELL OF THE TOAD WITH SEWN-UP EYES

Choose an older toad, which is male if the spell is for a man.

---

104 Translator's note: The following charms with toads, fern seeds, bats, etc. are also published in Humberto Maggi, *The Book of Saint Cyprian: The Great Book of True Magic*, Nephilim Press, 2018: 259–283.

After you are sure of it,[105] take it with your right hand and pass it under your belly five times, mentally saying the following words:

Toad, toad, just as I pass you under my belly, so ... (the name of the person who you want to bewitch) does not have peace or rest until he comes to me with all his heart and with all his body, soul and life.

Having said these words, take a needle of the greatest fineness and thread with a green silk strand, sewing with it the eyelids of the toad's eyes, taking great care not to damage the pupils, because otherwise, the person whom you want to enchant would be blind. Only the skin that surrounds the eyes is sewn, from bottom to top, so that the toad remains with its eyes hidden, but without having suffered any damage.

WORDS THAT ARE SAID TO THE TOAD AFTER HAVING SEWN THE EYES

"Toad: I, by the power of Lucifer and the prince Belzebuth, have sewn your eyes, which is what I should do to ... (the name of the person is said here), so that he has no peace or rest anywhere in the world without my company, and he is blind to all women (or men, depending on the sex of the person who you are trying to bewitch). See only me, and in me alone have your thoughts.

"So-and-so (pronounce the person's name), here you are imprisoned and tied up without seeing the sun or the moon, until you love me. From here I will not let you go; here you are captive, prisoner, as is this toad."

The pot or vessel in which the toad is placed must contain a little water, which will be renewed every day with some fresh.

---

105 Translator's note: i.e., that it is male.

SPELL WITH A TOAD THAT HAS A SEWN MOUTH

Take a large toad[106] and sew the mouth with a string of black silk, and after the mouth is sewn up, say the following words:

"Toad: I, by the power of Lucifer, Belzebuth and Astaroth,[107] and by that of all infernal spirits, I condemn you, So-and-so (here the name of the person you are trying to enchant is said), that you do not have even one hour of health, because I place your life inside the mouth of this toad, and just as he will die little by little, and lose his life along with his health, so it will happen to you by the power of Lucifer, of Belzebuth, of Astaroth and of all the infernal spirits."

It must be borne in mind that if, after the spell is actually done and when it has begun to take effect, you regret it, you can easily undo it, just by removing the toad from the pot, unstitching its mouth and giving it cow's milk to drink for five days.

When removed from the pot, the following words should be said:

"By the power of Lucifer, Belzebuth, Astaroth and all the infernal spirits, it is my will that the spell that weighed on so-and-so ... (here the name) be undone and that they regain health through my wishes, just as this toad is going to get it back through my care."

---

106 Both in this spell and in the previous one, the sex of the toad should be the same as that of the person against whom the spell is made.

107 Translator's note: The three infernal princes, they are evoked in the tradition of the most infamous grimoires, e.g. *The Grand Grimoire: A Practical Manual Of Diabolic Evocation And Black Magic*, Trident Books, 2004 and *The Grimoirum Verum*, edited and translated by Joseph Peterson, CreateSpace Publishing, 2007: 11–12.

SPELL OF THE TOAD TO BE LOVED AGAINST THE WILL
OF PEOPLE AND TO MAKE MARRIAGES

Suppose that a woman in love wanted to marry her boyfriend, or the person she loves, no matter what, within a short time, even if he is not [in love with her]; suppose also that the individual whom the woman wants to marry or to join her remains not only cold, but reluctant, because he does not want marriage or union.

His hesitation can be reduced, and first his ideas and then his feelings made to change, proceeding as follows:

Take an object of the lover and wrap it around the belly of the toad, and after this operation, tie the feet of the toad with a red ribbon, putting it inside a pot with earth mixed with some cow's milk. After practicing all these operations, say the following words, taking care to put your face in the mouth of the pot.

"So and so (say the name of the person), as long as this toad is imprisoned in this pot without seeing the sun or the moon, so you shall not see any woman, neither married, nor single nor widowed. You will have to fix your thoughts only on me, and just as this toad has tied legs, so yours are imprisoned and you cannot direct them except towards my house, and just as this toad lives inside this pot, consumed and mortified, so will you live as long as you do not marry or unite [with me]."

Having said these words, the pot is covered very well so that the toad does not see the clarity of the day; later, when you have achieved your wish, release the toad, take away the object that you wrapped around his belly without hurting him, and take good care of him, understanding that, otherwise, the person would suffer the same discomfort as the toad. This operation, the man can do the same as the woman.

TO MAKE AND UNDO AN EVIL SPELL

Take a black toad and sew its mouth with black silk. Then tie, one by one, the limbs or digits[108] of the toad with threads of black wool, and making like a parachute take the main thread of the wool, and hang it in the fireplace so that the toad is with its belly up. At twelve o'clock at night the devil (Lucifer) shall be called at each of the chimes of the clock, and then, turning the toad, say the following words:

"Unclean creature, by the power of the devil, to whom I sold my body and not my spirit, I order you not to let ... (the person's name) enjoy a shadow of happiness on earth. I place his health inside the mouth of this toad and just as it has to die, so also dies... (the name) whom I conjure three times in the name of the devil, the devil, the devil."

The next morning put the toad in a clay pot and cover tightly.

To undo the effects of this spell, assuming that the person suffered too much as a result of the spell, remove the toad from the pot and have it drink fresh cow's milk for seven days, after having unstitched its mouth.

TO MAKE A MAN DISLIKE HIS WOMAN OR THE WOMAN WITH WHOM HE LIVES, OR VICE VERSA

Choose a toad,[109] beautiful and young, and sew its eyes with black silk, being careful—as it already is indicated in the previous recipes—, not to hurt the pupil. Once this operation has been carried out, proceed in the same way as in the previous

---

108 Translator's note: "dedos".

109 We have already said that if the spell is for a *man*, the toad should be male, and if for a woman, *female*.

recipe, substituting the words that were uttered in that recipe with the following:

"Filthy creature![110] In the name of the devil, to whom I sold my body, but not my soul, I sewed your eyes, which I should have done with So-and-so (here the person's name), so that ... (he or she) likes no other person than me, and walks blindly regarding all other women or men."

The toad is then suspended from the kitchen chimney for twelve hours, then, if it remains alive, is placed in a hermetically covered bowl or clay pot.

The words that will be said when enclosing the toad in the pot will be the following:

"So and so ... (the person's name) you are here imprisoned and tied up and you will not see the light of the sun or the light of the moon until you love me with all your heart. Stay there, devil, devil, devil."[111]

In this as in the other recipes in which nothing has been indicated, the water that the toad must have should be refreshed daily.

RECIPE TO RUSH MARRIAGES

Take a black toad and tie around its belly two ribbons, one red and the other black, which ribbons will be used to hold to said belly an object belonging to the person you want to enchant, and insert it into a clay pot at once, saying these words:

"So-and-so (the person's name), if you love someone other than me, or dedicate your thoughts to another, the devil to whom I entrust my luck, will lock you up in the world of afflictions, in

---

110 Translator's note: "Bicho inmundo!".
111 Translator's note: "diablo, diablo, diablo".

the same way that I just locked up this toad, from where you will not leave except to marry me."

After saying these words, cover the pot tightly, refreshing the toad daily with the water that is essential for its life. The day on which the marriage is set, he will be released, taking care to leave him near a pool of water and not to mistreat him, otherwise, the marriage would take place but life would become unbearable for both spouses.

TO CAUSE THE EVIL EYE

Take two male lion eyes and put them to ventilate in the light of the crescent moon. When they are well aired, infuse them with some peppercorns in a bottle of aged white wine, which you will leave when the moon is in its first quarter. Once the aforementioned infusion has been verified, you will filter the wine through a very fine and pure linen cloth, and add a tablespoon of honey. Afterwards, you will remain locked in a room where the light does not penetrate for twenty-four hours, after which, you will drink a small glass of the concoction, raising your spirit and pronouncing these words:

"Lucifer, Belzebuth, Astaroth, lend me your infernal power against ... (here you will pronounce the name of the person you want to inflict the curse on). Amen."

Then you will go in search of her, with downcast eyes and trying not to look directly at people to whom you do not want to cause harm, and when you find her, you will look at her face for a few minutes, mentally exclaiming:

"By your virtue, Lucifer, Belzebuth, Astaroth, may my wish be granted! ... Amen."

It is proven that if this experiment is carried out in the way indicated, the person against whom you have directed yourself will immediately suffer the effects of your curse.

RECIPE TO FIND A WOMAN

Saint Cyprian says, that first of all, it is convenient to study the character and inclinations of the woman that is intended, in order to regulate the norm of conduct that must be observed in relation to the desires that want to be satisfied with her, not being less convenient to take into account that women pay a lot for the good appearance and better bearing of the person who wants to obtain their favors.

Observing this first condition, and after having declared one's intentions to love and serve her to the woman that one wishes, take the heart of a virgin pigeon and have it be eaten by a snake; after more or less time, the snake will die.

When this happens, cut off the head and dry it over low heat, or on a hot iron plate, and after drying, reduce it to powder, crushing it in a mortar and pestle, and after having added a few drops of laudanum[112] to the powder, when you want to use it, you will have to rub your hands with that preparation, immediately grasping those of your beloved.

RECIPES FOR MAN TO SURRENDER TO WOMEN'S WISHES

In addition to the first indications that we wrote down in the previous recipe, such as studying the temperament, genius and inclinations of the person whom it is desired to subjugate, and to dress with elegance and cleanliness, the woman will try to obtain from the man she chose, a coin, a medal, pin, object or piece of

---

112 Translator's note: A tincture of opium.

an object provided it is made of silver and that the man has worn it for at least twenty-four hours. Once this has been obtained, the suitor must approach the man, holding the silver object in her right hand and offering him with the other a glass of wine, into which a pill the size of a grain of millet, made with the following ingredients, will have first been dropped:

Eel's head, one.

Hemp seeds, whatever fits on your fingertips.

Laudanum, two drops.

After the man has, perforce, drunk this wine, he will also, perforce, love the woman who gave it to him, not being able to avoid her while the charm lasts, the effects of which can always be renewed without any inconvenience.

However, if the man is so strong that he resists the medicine or that it does not act with the desired promptness and effectiveness, the woman should invite him to drink chocolate in tea or coffee, in which she will mix the ingredients that are expressed below:

Powdered cinnamon, two fingers.

Cloves,[113] five.

Vanilla, quarter of a pod.

Scraped nutmeg, whatever will fit on your fingertips.

Immediately after putting in the cloves, they will be extracted, replacing them with two drops of tincture of cantaridas.[114]

When the woman is not in a great hurry to secure and seize the man, the first indicated preparation will suffice, without resorting to the tincture of cantaridas.

We will not hide that the man, when savoring the tea, coffee or chocolate, may notice that they have a somewhat strange taste, which—when the woman realizes and wishes—,

---

113 Translator's note: "Dientes de clavo".

114 Translator's note: This refers to substances produced by the *Lytta* (formerly *Cantharis*) *vesicatoria* beetle, a.k.a. Spanish Fly or Blister Beetle.

could be attributed to causes other than the good seasoning of the substances of reference, such as, for example, adulterations suffered by articles in stores, etc., etc.

When the woman—generally endowed with greater penetration and insight than the man—, suspects that he escapes her, either because another steals from her, or because he has begun to look at her with suspicion, the first step of antipathy, if she wants to retain him and to regain control over him, proceed as follows.

She will repeat her medicine every fifteen days, and in the intervals, inviting him to lunch or dinner, she will give:

At lunch, an omelette prepared in the following way: beat the eggs very well, adding two drops of tincture of cantaridas to them, and toss the beaten eggs from one bowl to another, saying: "Pass this fire that devours me to the heart of …[his name] as these eggs pass from one bowl to another." Repeating this operation three times, the omelette is made and served hot.

At lunch you will give him meatballs to eat, taking care to rub them one by one on your sweaty body, then passing them over your chest and belly, and holding them for a moment under your armpit. Then you will serve him virgin pigeons, roasted or fried swallows.

At both meals, you will present him with a cup of good coffee, strained through the tail of a shirt with which the woman must have slept for at least two nights.

AGAINST LOVE

If you want to stop loving a person unworthy of your affection, take the following philter: on Monday, when the moon is waning, at midnight, after the rooster with its song has driven away the infernal spirits, leave the house and go to the shore of a stream, a pond, or the sea, put your bare feet in its waters, and then, with them still wet, you will collect three circe flowers, saying when you take each one: *Phebus geneaen*[115] *you remedy of love between us.* Later you will return home before the rooster crows again and you will put the three flowers in a bottle, with half a spoonful of good white vinegar, and you will place that bottle for thirteen nights in a window under the influence of the stars, and during this time you will perform an extremely rigorous fast, and you will abstain from taking fermented liquors or others; on the thirteenth day you will put three tablespoons of honey collected in autumn into the flask, and add a large glass of water from the body that is close to the place where you picked the flowers, and every morning while fasting, you will take this philter pronouncing with all your willpower the magic words mentioned above, and then you will try to find the person you love, and without looking at her or touching her, you will dispute with her and stop loving her.

AGAINST PHILTERS

Any person who loves another by the influence of some philter, who takes the same shirt they have worn during their love affair with two hands and put their head through the right sleeve, you are instantly free of the curse.

---

115 Translator's note: A type of wine from Argentina.

Chapter II

Enchantments Produced by the Fern Seed and its Properties

THE CHARMS that are produced by means of the fern seed are extremely wonderful, as it will be seen later, provided that the prescriptions established by the ancient magicians, and particularly Saint Cyprian, are observed to take it.

At the festival of Saint John, at the first chimes of twelve o'clock, you will place a towel or a white linen cloth under a fern bush that you must have already chosen in advance and blessed in the name of the Father, the Son and of the Holy Spirit,[116] so that the devil cannot take over the plant.

Having carried out these operations, which could be called preliminary, you will draw a certain circle around the fern, placing the people who attend this ceremony within it.

The people who claim the seed of the fern having been placed within said circle, they must say the *litany* aloud to force the devil to withdraw, who will undoubtedly intend to scare the attendees, so that they do not achieve their purpose; but upon hearing the litany, which will be precisely that of the saints, all the demons will withdraw from that place. Once the litany is over, the seeds will be distributed proportionally to each one, without any disputes, otherwise the seed will lose all its virtue.

---

116 Translator's note: A Christian reference as compared to the Hebrew tradition of the infernal princes in the previous chapter.

WORDS EVERYONE SHOULD SAY LOOKING AT THE SEED
OF THE FERN

"Fern seed that was acquired at the festival of Saint John at midnight on the dot. You were obtained and placed on top of a talisman, for which you must serve for all sorts of incantations, and just as God is the divine point of Jesus, and Jesus is the human point of Saint John, so also every person by whom you are touched is enchanted with me.

"All this will be accomplished by the power of the great Almighty God, by whom I ... (here is the name of the person who makes the invocation), call you and I summon you so that you will not fail me, by the blood shed by Our Lord Jesus Christ, by the power and virtue of Maria Santisima,[117] may it be with me and with you. Amen."

At the end of these words, the Creed will be prayed making the cross over the seed, and at the end, the cross on that one (on the seed).

In this way, the seed is left with all its power and virtue, then passed through a flow of holy water.

Once all this is done, the seeds are put in a small bottle, covering them very well.

EXPLANATION OF THE VIRTUES AND WONDERS WITH
WHICH THE FERN SEED IS ENDOWED

1. Any person who obtains this seed, if he touches another person with malicious intent, will sin mortally, for having used a divine mystery to make offenses against humanity, as well as if he should touch a married or single woman to lead her to any place with malicious intent.

117 Translator's note: The Virgin Mary.

2. Any person who touches a fellow man with this seed in order to paralyze their action in affairs or business shall incur the penalty of excommunication.

3. The seed has virtue against any evil spirit that has taken possession of a person that is pleasing to us, for which it will be enough to touch them with said seed, putting all one's faith in Our Lord Jesus Christ.

4. Touching with it, with the same faith, a person who is ill, he will be healed, whatever the illness he suffered.

5. The seed has the effectiveness of defending us from the common enemy and his cunning, bringing us to our true knowledge.

6. The mind has a hidden virtue that works through an almost divine power, acting in the following way: suppose that a young woman sympathizes with a certain individual, but not with us. It is very easy to make said young woman sympathize with the one with whom she previously did not sympathize. In this case it will proceed as follows: when you are talking to her, touch her with three grains of the seed that concerns us, and you will have enchanted her from then on.

7. When you want a person to follow you, touch them with the seed and they will follow you to the end of the world, and when you want them to stop following you, touch them again in the same way.

8. There are so many properties and virtues that this seed has, that only the person who possesses it will be able to inform you.

In summary: the seed of the fern has virtue above all that the human being can want.

Chapter III

To Obtain the Protection and Help of the Demon Without Making a Covenant With Him

MAGIC OF THE BEANS

YOU WILL kill a black cat precisely on Saturday at the first stroke of twelve, and you will bury it in a field near your house, after having put a *bean* in each eye, another under the tail and another in each ear. Once all this is done, cover the cat with dirt, and water it every night at midnight with very little water, until the beans have sprouted and are ripe. When this happens, cut it down and take it home; then put the beans to dry, to make use of them when you see fit. Placing a bean in the mouth has the virtue of making you invisible and, therefore, you can penetrate anywhere without being seen. Placing it in the palm of the left hand and pressing it with the middle finger, and ordering the devil to introduce himself, he will present himself to you, immediately placing himself at your command.

Keep in mind that when you go to water the beans, many ghosts will appear to you in order to scare you and prevent your attempt. The reason for this is very simple; the devil does not like to put himself at the service of anyone if they have not previously given themself to him in body and soul. Do not be scared, therefore, when he presents himself to you, because he cannot do you wrong, for which occasion you must first of all make the sign of the cross and pray the Creed.

MAGIC WITH A BONE FROM THE HEAD OF A BLACK CAT

Boil a kettle of water with white willow wood, and when it is about to come to a boil, put a live black cat inside it, letting it cook until the bones are removed from the meat.[118] Once this operation has been carried out, dry all the bones with a cloth of linen, and place the person who is doing this in front of a mirror, putting bone by bone in their mouth until the image of the person who performs this operation disappears from the mirror, which will mean that this is the bone that has the virtue of making the person invisible who carries it in their mouth. When you want to go somewhere without being seen, you put the bone in your mouth and say: "I want to be in such a place by the power of black magic."

It should be noted that there is no need to insert the entire bone into the mouth to do the mirror test, it is enough to squeeze it a little with your teeth.[119]

ANOTHER CHARM BY VIRTUE OF BLACK CATS

When a black cat is together with a female cat of the same color for intercourse, get ready with a pair of scissors and cut a handful of hair from both of them. Then you will gather these and burn them with rosemary from the North, and together with the ash you will put a few drops of ammonia salt spirit in a glass jar, covering the jar well so that the spirit is always strong.

Once the preparation is done, you will take the jar with your right hand and say the following words:

"Ashes, that by my own hands were burned and that with steel scissors were cut from the cats, everyone who smells you is

118 A cat tucked into a bag or tightly tied diving basket.
119 Translator's note: See Appendix.

enchanted. This by the power of God and of Maria Santisima, his mother. And should God stop being God and this thing fail me, you will see yourself upset or dead, mutilated or one-eyed."

Complete this ceremony, concentrate all your willpower in the bottle, so that it acquires all the magical power that you desire, and when the occasion comes for you to give it to smell, as if it were a fragrant water, to the person you would like to enchant, they will bend to your will as the reed bends to the wind.

TO GET REVENGE ON A PERSON AND CAUSE HIM EVIL

When you want to take revenge on a declared enemy, and have him be ignorant of your revenge, you can do the following:

You will tie up a black cat that does not have a single white hair, by the hind legs as well as the front, with a length of rope.

Once this operation is carried out, you will take the cat tied in the indicated way to some of the most solitary forest or crossroads that you can find, and there you will say the following:

"I ... (here one's own name should be said), on behalf of Almighty God, command the devil to appear to me, on pain of disobedience to the superior precepts. I, by the power of liberal black magic, command you, oh demon! Lucifer or Satan, that you enter into the body of ... (here the name of the person to whom you want to do evil is said), to whom I wish to cause evil, and also order you, in the name of that same omnipotent God, that you do not withdraw from his body while I have nothing to order you to do, and do for me everything that I wish, and it consists of ... (here is said what you want the devil to do).

"Oh great Lucifer! Emperor of all that is infernal, I catch you and stop you, and I tie you in the body of ... (So-and-so), in the same way that I have this black cat imprisoned and tied. In order for you to do everything I want, I offer you this black cat, and that I will hand over to you when you have carried out my mandates."

When the demon has fulfilled his obligation, you go to the place where you made the spell and say to him twice in a row: "Lucifer, Lucifer, here is what I promised you", and then release the cat.

WAY TO GET TWO DEVILS WITH THE EYES OF A BLACK CAT

You will kill a black cat that does not have a single white or gray hair, and after having removed the eyes, you will put them inside two eggs laid by a black hen, taking care that each eye must be separated in each egg. After this operation is done, you will put them, perfectly hidden, inside a pile of horse manure, noting that it is necessary that the manure is kept very warm while the imps are generated.

Saint Cyprian says that one must go to the manure heap every day for a month, which is the time it takes for the little devils to be born.

In the visit that must be made daily to the manure that encloses both eggs, in which they will be engendering the devils, the following words should be said, as a prayer:

"Oh great Lucifer! I give you these two eyes of a black cat, so that you, my great friend Lucifer, be favorable to me in the supplication that I make at your feet. My great minister and friend Satanas, to you I give black magic so that you can put in it all your power, efficacy and cunning with which the Supreme Being endowed you, and that you dedicate to the damage and harm of humans, so I entrust to you these two eyes of a black cat so that two little devils will be born from them, which will accompany me eternally. I give my black magic to Maria Padilla, to all her family and to all the devils of hell, maimed, blind and crippled, so that from here two little devils will be born to supply me with money, because I want money by the power of Lucifer, my friend and partner from now on."

You do everything that is said, and at the end of a month, a day more, a day less, to you will be born two imps that will have the figure of a small lizard. Once the birth is done, put them inside an ivory or boxwood tube and you will feed them iron or steel filings.

Once you are in possession of these monsters of hell, you can do whatever you want and, for example, if you want money, just open the tube and say: "I want money", which will appear to you immediately, but with the sole condition that you will not be able to give it as alms to the poor, nor to have masses said, because it is money from the devil.

Chapter IV

Spells by Means of a Bat

THE BAT has been one of the animals that primitive magicians used to enchant people.

When you want to use it, you will do it in the following way and for the cases indicated.

TO MAKE HIM LOVE

Let us suppose that a young woman or any woman wishes to marry a certain person, as briefly as possible, then she must work in the following way:

Provide yourself with a bat and pass a needle with a strong thread through its eyes. Once this operation has been carried out, both the needle and the thread have acquired the power of a spell and will be used by making five points in the shape of a cross with it, on an object that belongs to the person to be enchanted, pronouncing the following words:

"So-and-so[120] (the name will be said) I enchant you by the power and strength of Luzbel,[121] Belzebuth and Astaroth, so that you do not see the sun or the moon, as long as you do not marry me. Therefore, I conjure you to do so within the non-extendable period of eight days, on pain of resorting to other more powerful spells. Luzbel, Belzebuth, Astaroth, confirm my

---

120 Translator's note: "Fulano o Fulana", i.e. the masculine and feminine forms of the generic proper noun.

121 Translator's note: Another name of Lucifer.

wish and oblige ... (the name is stated here) to subjugate himself body and soul to mine."

Once all this has been executed and the person is enchanted, they will not have an instant of calm, while they do not join the one who produced the spell.

If later you do not want to join the person you enchanted, you must burn the object with which the spell was made.

ANOTHER FORMULA TO DO THE SAME

Kill two bats, male and female, so that you can take advantage of their blood, which you will mix, adding a few drops of ammonia salt spirit, putting all this in a glass bottle of convenient dimensions, so that you can always carry it in the pocket.

When you want to bewitch a young woman, just as when she wants to bewitch a man, it is enough to give her a smell of the contents of the bottle.

SPELL THAT CAN BE MADE WITH MALLOWS COLLECTED IN A CEMETERY OR IN THE ATRIUM OF A CHURCH

Take three clumps of hollyhocks,[122] take them with you and put them under the mattress of the bed where you sleep, saying every day when you wake up:

"So-and-so ... (say the name of the person against whom the spell is directed), just as these hollyhocks were found in the cemetery and underneath me they are placed, so you will remain prisoner by the power of Lucifer and magic, and only when the bodies of the cemetery or the church see and find these hollyhocks that grew by virtue of their oils, will you leave me."

---

122 Translator's note: "malvas", i.e. flowers of the *Malvaceae* family, including hollyhock, commonly known as mallows.

These words must be repeated with force of will for nine consecutive days, in order to produce the desired effect.

Part Four

THE SECRETS OF QUEEN CLEOPATRA

Chapter I

Recipes and Ointments

FOR A WOMAN TO KEEP HER BEAUTY

EVERY MORNING, take fresh and lean veal meat, which has been slaughtered in the hour when the sun dominates; cut it into small slices and place it on the face and on the other parts of the body that you would like to be kept in a state of freshness, and leave it on those parts for an hour.

TO KEEP THE SKIN FINE AND PLEASANT TO THE TOUCH

Take the liquor called *cytisa* water, and leave it exposed to the influences of the Moon, Mars and Venus, in an uncovered pot, for three or four nights, and then, for twenty-four hours, under the sun. Then you will add a few drops of fresh cow's or goat's milk, donkey's being preferable, and you will wash the parts of the body that you want to whiten and polish with that mixture.

MANNER OF WHITENING THE SKIN

Brunette women will bathe frequently to whiten their skin, and wash their faces every day with a few drops of wine spirit, mixed with virgin milk and with distilled bean flower water.

INFUSION FOR THE SKIN

Infuse *rabanus* flower,[123] then mix it with milk and wash your face every night with this simple composition.

PREPARATION TO REMOVE SKIN ERUPTIONS

Squeeze leek juice, mix it with an equal amount of lightly sweetened milk or cream, and use this mixture to wash the parts that are grainy, the rash of which will disappear in a short time.

OINTMENT AGAINST WRINKLES

Take:

White lily onion juice ..... 2 oz.
White honey .... 2 oz.
Melted white wax .... 1 oz.

Incorporate the whole and after, mixing the indicated ingredients well, make an ointment with which you will rub your face every night at bedtime.

---

123 Horseradish.

BEAUTY BATH

Take two pounds of hulled barley, one pound of rice, three pounds of powdered *lupinum*,[124] eight pounds of bran, and ten handfuls of borage and violets and cook everything in sufficient quantity of river water and pass the resulting liquor through a sieve, said liquor to be made use of at will.

This bath is perfect to beautify and soften the skin.

AGAINST INFLAMMATION AND RED CONGESTION OF THE EYELIDS

There is nothing that affects the face more than the inflammation and reddish congestion of the eyelids. How many young people, truly beautiful and pleasant, have lost, for that reason, a good marriage!

To combat this terrible inflammation, something that is easy to recognize by the increase in volume of the eyelids and even more so by the reddish color that the eyelids acquire, it is necessary, firstly, to protect the eyes from light and then wash them three times a day with rose water of superior quality, mixed with water that has been boiled for half an hour. The washing must be done with a very fine linen cloth.[125] Some physicians also advise a rose borate and zinc acid ointment, which should only be used in very persistent or already chronic cases.

---

124 Lupins.

125 At present what our most famous oculists use is a solution of boric acid using sterilized hydrosium cotton and not using the same cotton twice.

FOR THE BEAUTY OF THE EYES

The length of the eyelashes and their abundance is one of the main causes of the beautification of the eyes, since they darken and enlarge them, making them appear more dreamlike, more ideal, at the same time increasing the charms of the physiognomy.

How to get this? Very easily: it is enough to cut the tips of the eyelashes during a three-quarters waxing moon, using very fine and curved scissors, giving said eyelashes, after washing the eye and its accessories well with a boric solution, a light rubbing with sweet almond oil. Once this operation is carried out in the indicated way, you will see how the eyes acquire, due to the length and abundance of the eyelashes, a shadow that will make them appear larger and blacker, even when the pupil is not this color.

TO MAKE THE BAGS THAT FORM UNDER THE EYES DISAPPEAR

No matter how beautiful, large and slanted they may be, the bags that usually form under them, an appendage or attachment that is an indication of fatigue, if not old age, makes the interest of the beautiful in the disappearance of those bags even greater.

To achieve this result, it is enough to undergo a wisely practiced massage that, however simple it may be, it will be advisable to always entrust it to a practical person.

TO MAKE THE MARKS LEFT BY SMALLPOX DISAPPEAR FROM THE FACE

Smallpox is an evil caused by the planet Mars. The person who wishes that the traces this terrible disease leaves upon him disappear from his face, will take at the time of the Moon,

Mercury, Saturn or Jupiter, its enemies, in proportionate quantity, litharge, dried cane root, chickpea flour and rice flour, and after mixing and pulverizing everything well, add sweet almond oil and melted mutton tallow, smearing this mixture on your face before going to bed and washing it in the morning when you get up with warm rather than hot water. This operation can be repeated as many times as you want, taking care not to do it when the planet Mars dominates in the heavens.

FOR THE RHEUMA[126]

You will crush and powder a couple dozen hot, dry chillies.

Once this is done, you will put half a liter of pure olive oil on the fire, and when it is ready you will add the chilli powder, frying it well and stirring this mixture for a while with a spatula or wooden spoon.

When it has cooled down, you will keep it in a jar or bottle, and to use it you will put it to heat a little in a cup and rub the sore part, immediately covering it with a very hot cloth. This remedy should be used every twelve hours, until the pain disappears.

FOR INFLAMMATIONS

When you have a leg or arm swollen and sensitive, take fresh nettles and massage it with them, for five minutes, then covering the swollen diseased part with a hot cloth. Using this remedy every twelve hours, you will soon notice that the inflammation subsides.

---

126 Translator's note: Rheumatoid arthritis.

ANOTHER FORMULA FOR RHEUMA

Put in a bottle essential oil of turpentine, 15 grams; opodeldoc liquid balm,[127] 60 grams. Once this is done, you will shake it well to mix it.

To use it, heat it slightly and rub the painful part, covering it with a hot cloth.

FOR BURNS

You will take a little quicklime and put it in water for two hours. When it has settled and the water turns out, although slightly white, quite clear, it is removed by decantation,[128] preventing the lime from escaping.

This water is mixed with fresh lard, working it well, as if making an ointment.

Then you will keep it in a cup, and when you have to use it you will spread a little of the grease on a linen cloth and apply it to the burn, tying it over with a bandage.

Every three hours a new treatment can be made, until the ill is over.

---

127 Translator's note: A medical plaster or liniment invented—or at least named—by the German Renaissance physician Paracelsus in the sixteenth century. In its modern form opodeldoc is a mixture of soap in alcohol, to which camphor and sometimes a number of herbal essences, most notably wormwood, are added.

128 Translator's note: A common example of decantation is oil and vinegar. When a mixture of the two liquids is allowed to settle, the oil will float on top of the water so the two components may be separated.

RECIPE AGAINST WARTS

Dissolve baking soda in a little water, as much as it can take.

The warts are soaked with this water for two minutes, at sunset and sunrise, and it is said: "Go away, wart, since the sun takes you away", and repeat for three days.

ANOTHER TO GET THEM

On a serene night in January, three stars will be counted, saying when looking at them: "One, two, three, little wart, come." During this ceremony, a pinch will be given in the part where you want the wart to come out. It is repeated three nights in a row, taking great care to always direct the view to the same stars.

By doing this with true desire, you will soon see the wart form.

TO REMOVE THE FRECKLES

A little raw cotton is soaked in hydrogen peroxide and applied for five minutes on the freckles to be removed.

In case of skin irritation, wash with a 4% boric acid solution.

DEPILATORY[129] RECIPE

The ancient magicians say that the brains of the eagle, well crushed and macerated for a few days in alcohol or ether, make the locks and body hair of the person who rubs himself with this mixture fall out. In the *untuariums* of Rome in the time of Nero, such an ointment, made exclusively by the Capuan people, was an indispensable article for waxing, especially among hairy women.

---

129 Translator's note: Hair removal.

MEDICINAL VIRTUES OF PRECIOUS STONES

Jonas Sufurino says, in his fourth part of the work, that the stones are inductile earthly bodies, set by a lapidifying virtue, of lapidescent matter, that is, viscous, terrestrial or infernal, and that they are generated from the terrestrial saline peritoma, which results in and congeals into the hardness of stone, by its lapidistic virtue. All stones, Jonas adds, have their respective virtues, some being more precious than the others.

The main preparations that are made with them for the various medicinal uses that will be indicated are the following: pulverization, calcination, solution, coagulation, purification or sweetening, liquefaction, distillation or volatilization, to which sirupization is added.

With these preparations, the precious stones are placed in a position to utilize them in the uses indicated, such as salts, specifics (magisterium), liquor oils, tinctures or essences. After these general explanations comes the particular detail for each *gemstone* in the following way:

TOPAZ

The faculties and virtues of this stone, given its nature, solar by signature, are: reduction of nocturnal tumors; melancholy, comforting of understanding and opposition to annoying daydreams, carrying it tied to the left arm or pendant from the neck, within a gold frame.

GARNET

There are western and eastern ones, the latter being the best. They have the virtue of drying out, corroborating, making the palpitations of the heart cease; resisting moral illnesses; they are refractory to poison; they stop the sputum of blood and resolve the terrestrial in the body.

HYACINTH

Its faculties and virtues, especially those of the East, are the following: to corroborate (strengthen) the heart and preserve from the plague, being a particular specific against spasms and contractions. It is also considered a secret anti-pestiferant hanging around the neck or set in a ring.

NEPHRITE

This stone, opaque in nature, is either of mixed colors or a mixture of the color green with the others, rarely being two colors, even though green always predominates in any of its various shades. It is highly recommended against kidney or stomach pain, and particularly against stone or sand disease, ailments that the stone cures by carrying it tied to an arm or a leg, or hanging from the neck.

RUBY

It is a sparkling gemstone with a color or hue very similar to that of blood; its goodness is tested with the mouth or the tongue. In this way it is known that the colder and harder they are, the better. As they are born between stony materials, at first they whiten, maturing little by little, until they contract that bloody hue.

Its main virtues, whether in drink or hanging around the neck, or set in a ring, are to resist poisons, and to preserve from the plague the one who will carry them, to correct sadness, restrain libidinal appetites, ward off bad thoughts and bad dreams and keep the body in its natural state. When misfortunes come upon man, he shows that he has lost the maturation of color and that he has become darker. After these [stones], it will be seen that he has recovered his color again. Its preparations are made in the same way as the other stones.

SAPPHIRE

It is transparent and diaphanous blue in color, which is sometimes white and sometimes properly blue. In the second case they are males, and females in the first. It is astringent, cordial and ophthalmic in character, which is why it dries the dampness of the eyes and blood: it corrects the inflammations produced by eye drops. Mixed with clarified butter and smearing the upper lids of the eyes with the mixture, it is valid and useful for all the fluxes[130] of the belly, for dysentery, hepatic flow, evacuations of blood in hemorrhoids, taking it with plantain or storm water. Heals ulcers and internal sores, corroborates the heart and makes it happy. It is a preservative against plague and poison and even evil fevers; heals any affection of the heart and melancholy, taking it internally. The whole sapphire, placed on the forehead, stops hemorrhages, and applied to inflammations, extinguishes them, and placed on the eyes removes everything that has fallen into them, preserving them from many ailments. Prepare in the common way; rinse it off well with warm water to make salt, liquor, oil, essence or tincture.

---

130 Translator's note: "proflubios".

EMERALD

It is a precious stone, diaphanous, transparent and very beautiful for its pleasant greenness, being more fragile than all other precious stones.

Its virtues consist in stopping all flow of the belly and blood, and mainly it is taken or given for dysentery, when it is doubted whether it comes from biting humors, or that it is born or originates from poison. Heals poisonous bites and plague. Its weight is six to ten grams. It is also effective for epilepsy, to accelerate labor, attaching it to the left thigh, and placed on the belly to retain it. It stops bleeding by placing it in the mouth.

Applied as salt and tincture, it cures dysentery and any other kind of flux, and is no less useful in the affections of the heart and the head, palpitations, sadness, frenzy, fainting, syncope, etc.

CORAL

Coral—shortening what Jonas [Sufurino] says about its color and sex—is male or female, a distinction that must be made for the uses indicated. It is male coral when its color is pure and genuinely red, and it is the one to be used when there is no mention of the hue. It is female coral that has a pale color, followed by black and white, which have no use in medicine.

Its virtues and efficacy are as follows:

All crushed coral cools and *astringes* mainly the heart, and in addition to this it corroborates the belly and cools the liver. As it purifies the blood, it is effective against the contagion of any disease, poison or malignant fever. It produces joy in the one who wears it with faith and knowledge of its virtue, when it is male. The blackish coral causes melancholy, stops the flows of the belly, uterus and ringworm; it preserves men from gonorrhea and children from epilepsy,[131] if ten grains are administered before drinking the mother's milk. Used as an external medicine, it is recommended for ulcers, for all kinds of healing and to stop tear production.

Their preparations are as follows:

The actual preparation is done in the common way. Calcination can be by *ignition* or *corrosion*. Calcination is sometimes softer and sometimes more violent, and if salt is desired, it will be necessary to reduce it to ashes by means of a very violent fire, that is, in the way that lime is obtained. Corrosion is done with saltpeter or stone and a sponge.

To dissolve the corals, purified common vinegar, May dew, spirit of honey and many others are used; and if the calcination had been with sulfur, it is dissolved with common water. The purification is done with distilled water or with well distilled May dew, or with some cordial water. It can also be done by distillation, evaporation or precipitation.

Coral liquor is made by descent[132] or distillation, its dose being four to twelve grains. The preparation of the essence is more laborious, but, on the other hand, its effectiveness is greater, administering from six to twelve drops of it.

LAPIS LAZULI

It has the ability to purge all melancholic affects, the quartan [fever], apoplexy, epilepsy, the vices of the spleen and many others that originate in the melancholic humor.

Wearing it around the neck corrects the spasms of children, strengthens the sight and preserves pregnant women from abortion and prevents fainting, it being warned that the woman who will

---

131 Translator's note: "alferecía".

132 Translator's note: "descenso", possibly referring to precipitation.

carry this stone must take it off when the delivery approaches, so that it does not prevent the exit of the fetus. One makes with lapis lazuli: a preparation against acrimony; an elixir against ulcers, an oil against foot pain and inflammation; an essence that is applied in doses of half a scruple, and a purgative salt.

AMBER

The best and most commonly used is gray.[133] The virtues of amber are the following: it warms, dries, resolves, fortifies the heart and brain and strengthens the vital and animal spirits with its sulphurous and gentle exhalation. Amber preparations are a great comfort to the internal parts and have the virtue of promoting procreation.

---

133 Translator's note: Probably a reference to ambergris.

Part Five

PHILOSOPHY OF MAGIC

THE CABALA AND THE UNKNOWN FORCES

Chapter One

The Ternary and the Immutable Laws of Nature

THERE ARE many neophytes who have asked me to explain why the laws of nature are immutable. I will answer them. If you go to the cabala, you will be able to observe that the Chaldean shepherds, before the priesthood of magic was exercised, recognized in principle the existence of three worlds: the *material world*, the *moral world* and the *divine world*, to which correspond: heaven, to the *divine world*; earth, to the *moral world*, and hell, a place of darkness, to the *material world*, ignorant and deprived of light. Knowing this, what worried the magicians then was the mystery of creation. Two persons in principle: the father and the mother, completed by the son. Thus, if the number *three* predominated in the worlds, the number three must also predominate in creation. The ternary was, therefore, for magic (as today is the trinity in Christian dogma) the harmonic dogma, the key to all sciences and all mysteries. Having observed that equilibrium is the universal law in physics and that it results from the apparent opposition of two forces marching from physical equilibrium (nature) to metaphysical equilibrium (above nature), they declared that in God, that is, the first cause living and active, two properties should be recognized, indispensable to each other: stability and movement balanced by the crown, that is, the supreme force.

And since they recognized in the sun the mystery of the ternary in unity, or three in one, for example: electricity, light and heat (the components of the sun), they conceived three persons in God and defined them in this way:

Kether: The supreme power, the incomprehensible, indefinable being, the being that is not in science, that does not exist in our intellectual reflection.

Chochmah: Wisdom, the ideal of sovereign reason, the ideal, whose most perfect imagining could only be a mirage.

Binah: Intelligence, freedom founded on the supreme order, the motive force of all movement, the cause of all initiative.

That is to say: the movement, which is the necessity of life and life itself, caused by the struggle between active intelligence and resistant wisdom, balanced by the supreme reason and represented by the triangle:

KETHER

la razón suprema, poder equilibrador

K

Binah, la inteligencia que se agita e impele hacia adelante.

Chochmah, la sabiduría que resiste.

B   *C*

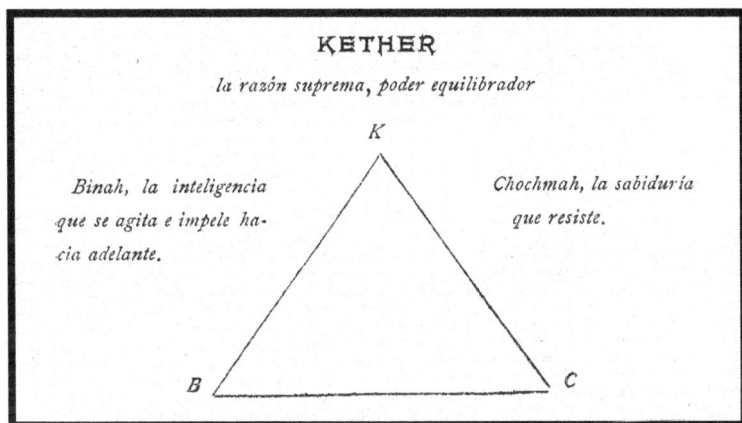

Nature, with its immutable laws, offers the incessant reflection sensed by magicians.

Chapter II

The Laws of Analogy According to the Sephirot

YOU ASK me, oh neophytes insatiable for knowledge! why, in addition to the immutable laws of nature, are there those of analogy? Observing the march of nature, it is not possible to doubt it.

Plants—Hermes has said symbolically—have the destiny of leading the grossest particles to a more perfect condition; they take the salts, the oil, the sulfur, they assimilate it and purify it, because their whole mechanism consists in raising the inferior substances to a superior state.

The growth of a creature is produced only by its own effort, repeated to yield to nature new organic powers, and these powers tend incessantly to take on new forms. All the lower beings seem to be heading in their march to take on new forms: towards the human form.

Can man back down?

Everything comes together in nature. If man is the highest link in the chain of terrestrial organization, he instead forms, in turn, the first link of another chain of a higher order, of which he is only an insignificant ring. Cabala itself, by showing us the guilty souls condemned to inhabit new bodies, does not admit each transformation of that body, except as a test to arrive, degree by degree, at purification, passing, if necessary, through degeneration and through the pain.

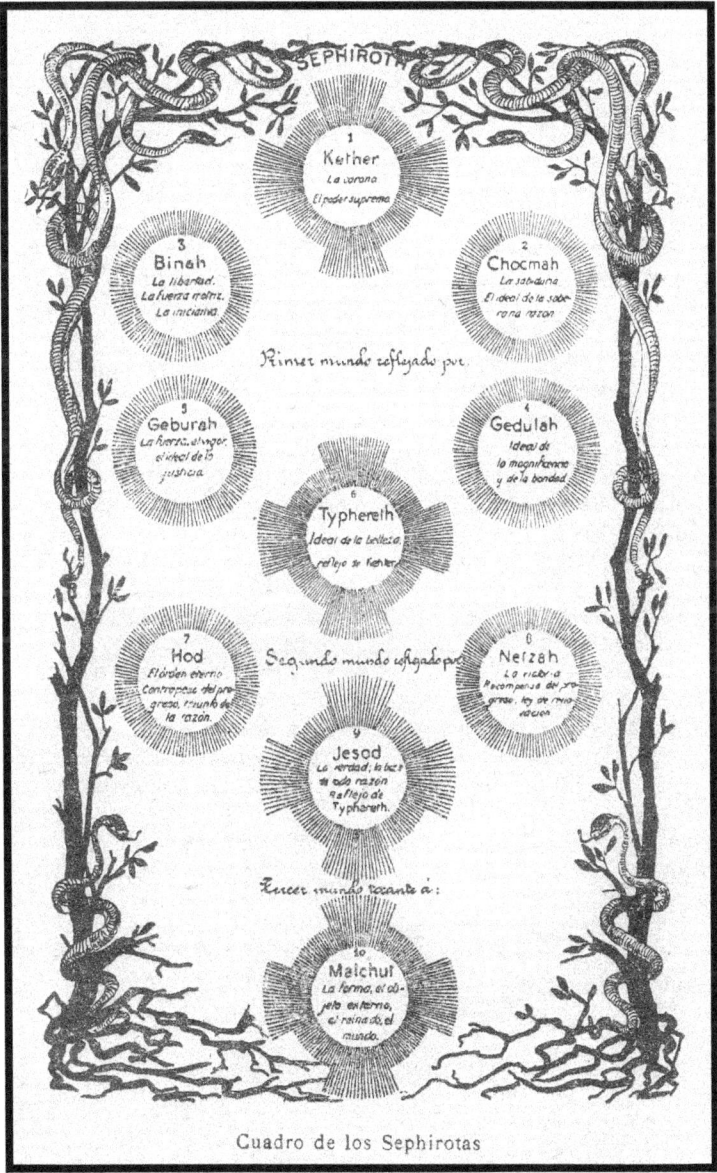

Cuadro de los Sephirotas

PICTURE OF THE SEPHIROT

The picture of the Sephirot, which we present here, is the pentacle of the three metaphysical worlds represented by three triangles successively descending from the creative light, from the ineffable being that no human imagination can conceive, down to our terrestrial world.

cabalists therefore recognize three suns: Ours, the sun of our system, is but a pale reflection of the other two. The sephirot are the emblem of the other superior worlds symmetrically placed in antagonism and in reflections downward like the reflection in water.

Thus *Kether*, the supreme being, has as a reflection *Typhereth*, beauty, and the reflection of beauty is truth, Jesod.

Chochmah, wisdom, resists *Binah*, the freedom that propels forward. But the wisdom of *Chochmah* is reflected by *Gedulah*, the ideal of goodness, God, love. Wisdom that resists is goodness that aspires to good.

Freedom, *Binah*, reflects rigor, *Geburah*, in antagonism with *Gedulah*, love. Thus it is freedom itself that calls for rigor and justice.

The ideal of goodness, when reflected, becomes *Netzah*, victory, which makes progress triumph by using it.

Rigor, when reflected, becomes *Hod*, the eternal order, because rigor regularizes freedom and uses its active principle for good.

Malchut is the result, the form, the domain; it is the world from which we begin to go back to God. Malchut is the universe, the entire creation, the work and the mirror of God.

Chapter III

Signifcance and Value of Numbers

IT WAS the ancient magicians who taught Pythagoras the system and significance of numbers. Effectively: the divine essence being inaccessible to the senses, we use to characterize it, not the language of the senses, but that of the spirit. We give intelligence or the *active* principle of the universe, the name of the *monad* and unity, because it is always the same; to matter, that is, to the *passive* principle, that of *dyad* or multiplicity, because it is subject to all sorts of changes; to the world, in short, that of *triad*, because it is the result of intelligence and matter. Whatever the mode, the system is presented and constituted by *Kether, Binah* and *Chochmah*: always the struggle between the active and the passive principle, from which movement is the source of life.

The sense of the lessons of the most ancient magicians about numbers is that they contain the elements of all things and even of all sciences.

Applying the number system to the world of spirits, Pythagoras solves problems completely unknown in our current arithmetic. Here is what a cabalistic sage has said about this matter:

The great system of the world rests on certain bases of harmony, of which the being, the form and the action of all things, both special and general, are a natural consequence. Those bases of harmony are called numbers. He who knows them, does not ignore the laws by which nature exists, the comparison of its relationships, the genus and the measure of its effect, the bond of union of all things and of all facts, physics and mechanics of the world. Numbers are the invisible bases of beings, in the same way that their bodies are the visible bases, that is, there is a double character of things, one visible and the other invisible. The visible is the visible form: that is to say, the body; the invisible form is the number. And everything that is presented or manifested is the result of an inner energy, and that energy is the unfolding of a force. The more or less great forces come from real numbers, and the more or less great energy from *virtual* numbers.

There are obviously invisible envelopes, because each being has a beginning and a form; but the principle and the form are two extremes that could never be united without a certain bond that would bring them closer together; this, then, is the function of the number. As the laws and qualities of beings are written on their exterior, the laws and qualities of invisible things are written upon invisible numbers: and just as impressions of the sensitivity of thought are received through the senses, so too our spirit receives lucid ideas of the position and the invisible destiny of things, as much as it can seize them. Because the ideal has, like the physical, number, measure and weight, whose position is only visible to the intelligence. The true numbers of the world are certainly infinite, but their course is simple and direct, since everything rests on the fundamental numbers from one to ten. Their infinity rests on the infinite and indeterminate number of beings themselves, and this all the more, as the same beings have greater classes of qualities. There are, then, numbers for the background and substance of beings, their effect, their duration, and the degrees of their progress (progression). All these things are so many stations where the rays of divine light stop and throw reflections backwards, both to represent their own image, and to bring to that same retrograde glance a new life, a new measure, a new weight. There are also numbers gathered to express the different relationships and the different positions of beings, their action and their effect. So while there are central numbers and circumference numbers; in the same way there are false numbers and impure numbers. Despite its infinite unity, the idea itself is extremely simple, because everything rises from the first fundamental figure up to ten, and the simple numbers, these resting again on the first *four* fundamental numbers, whose meeting (addition) gives 10, whence comes the inestimable force of the quaternary, which seems crazy to modern people, because they cannot understand any of it. We see in this very clearly why the number 4 was so highly sacred to the Pythagoreans, to the point of considering it a square ἀρρητόν. They swore by the number 4, this oath being the most sacred they could use. In it were enclosed all the symphonies and forces of nature. Ten was the number of the world or the absolute All (πᾶν). According to Pythagoras, numbers are the basis of the divine spirit and the only means by which things are shown; the union of all the assembled numbers of worlds, or the basis of the agreement of beings and their efforts, forms the harmony of the great whole. This is why Pythagoras looked at astrology and astronomy as two closely linked branches of the same science.

There is also a great difference between the numbers and the figures that can be counted; the former are *destinations* and consist only of spiritual greatness; the latter, on the contrary, have corporeal things as their object and are the visible expression of the invisible. All spiritual figures are rays, equations, effluvia of the unit, as *one* or the *unit* is the beginning of the figures that can be counted. One is also the name and the character of the highest great principle, of what is unique and infinite. One is the center of everything, the bottom of each being and of all the particular units that are not absolute and necessary, but that are mediate or immediate radiations of the absolute unit. Ten units form a unit of ten to one hundred; ten tens are the unit of one hundred, and so on. All the great units contain the small ones, they are contained in the greater ones, and thus the mutual set is produced. The very thing happens in nature. Each superior world contains all the subordinate units or the inferior worlds, and the smaller ones reciprocally take part in the superior worlds, spheres, figures or creatures, being in a class of subordinates contained in them. In the hundreds, for example, all numbers from one to one hundred are contained, and in the category of the *animal* are all the animals of creation; and as all the numbers from one to one hundred come closer and closer, so too the animals, even the lowest, rise in grade, always ascending and crossing, until their most distinguished members come to join man, although, nevertheless, unable to reach his height.[134]

The infinite deviation of the races of animals, descending from one to the other, also manifest the relations of number in the sense of the engendering unit of an infinity of spoils and remains. This enlightening method, coming from the East, corresponds to that by which, among the classes and the species, the lowest come out of the highest.

Not only the most famous philosophers, but also Catholic doctors, among others, Saint Jerome, Saint Augustine, Saint Origen, Saint Ambrose, Saint Gregory of Nazianzus, Saint Athanasius, Saint Basil, Saint Hilary, Saint Cyprian and others, assure that there is an admirable and effective virtue hidden in numbers.

Saint Cyprian affirms that everything that nature has created in principle, seems to have been formed by means of the numbers, since this has been the principle modeled on the spirit of the creator. This is where the quantity of elements comes from, that of the revolutions of time and the stars, the change of the sky and the state of numbers. Everything that is done subsists and has its virtue by numbers, because time is composed of numbers, and all that is movement and action is subject to time and movement.

---

134 It has taken more than two thousand years for modern naturalists, *even without having knowledge of these theories*, to reach an identical result, the retroaction that is noticed in the physical and natural sciences being due to these facts.

Cornelius Agrippa[135] and Saint Martin,[136] as well as Saint Cyprian, attained prophecy by means of the numbers. Here is what the last one says:

> The number is nothing other than the repetition of the unit. Unity easily penetrates all of the numbers and is the common mean of all of them, as it is their source and origin. There is thus *one* God, *one* world that belongs to God, *one* sun for the world, *one* phoenix in the world, *one* king among the bees, *one* chief in each army, *one* commander in each legion. There is *one* element that exceeds and penetrates everything: fire. There is a thing created by God, which is the object of the general admiration of beings, and which is on earth as well as in heaven; *it is the vegetable and mineral soul that is found everywhere, that nobody knows and that nobody calls by name,* but that is hidden under numbers, figures and enigmas, and without which neither alchemy nor natural magic could be successful. Number is therefore harmony, and without harmony nothing is possible.
>
> *Two* is antagonism, it is momentary immobility when forces are equal, but it is struggle, the beginning of movement. The number *two* is, therefore, essential, since

135 Translator's note: Heinrich Cornelius Agrippa (1486–1535), German polymath, author, physician, legal scholar, soldier, theologian and occultist.

136 Translator's note: The miracles of Saint Martín de Porres (1579–1639) included his almost clairvoyant knowledge of the procedure or medication necessary to treat a disease, the instantaneous healing of patients both in person and with the use of the gift of bilocation, and his famous ability to communicate with animals. There were several saints by the name of Martin in history, but this is the one most likely referred to here.

it represents the combined action of two *units*, that is, life, which can only be realized by action and movement. *Two*, therefore, is antagonism; but *three* is existence, it is the pendulum that, turning from left to right or vice versa, produces balance and with it movement.

Three is God: *vita, verbum, lux*; life, word, light. Here is the Trinity. The *Father is life*, and consequently power and strength, the character of this *life being expansion*. In the Son is the *word*, speech. But what is to be understood by the *word*? All the sages agree that it is *the form*. How is the Holy Spirit light? Light—it is said and we affirm it—is neither substance nor intelligence, but the result of their union; it is not composed of two, but it is half substance and half intelligence; it is in a certain way different from the one and the other, because it does not proceed by composition, but is simple in itself and indivisible, no more the one than the other, because light is everywhere where intelligence survives life, and if life and intelligence are infinite, light should also be.

Wisdom, who has always been regarded as the *divine Word*, son of God, speaks like this in *Proverbs*:

When He was preparing the heavens, I was there; when he gave the abyss a law and a limit; when he established the firmament and distributed with measure the springs of the waters; when he put a brake on the seas and established a law for their waves, so that they did not exceed their limits; when he laid the foundations of the earth, I was with him, arranging all things, delighting myself, rejoicing before him, enjoying the universe, and my delights would be none other than to always be with the children of men.

The number *three* is, therefore, the movement that forms the balance passing successively from one point to another; the number *four* is the perfect balance, it is the square, positivism, realism.

Four in magic is the cube, the square. It is the image of the earth; the quaternary is the consequence of the ternary; the ternary is the spirit, the movement, the resistance, which naturally led to the quaternary: stability, harmony.

For the ancient cabalists, the number four was the one that contained the four elements. The four astronomical cardinal points are, relative to us, the yes and no of light, the East and the West, the yes and no of heat; the South and the North, say the cabalists. The number four is also the cross.

Soon in the numbers 1, 2, 3, 4, was discovered, not only one of the principles of the musical system, but also those of physics and morals, all of them becoming proportion and harmony: time, justice, friendship, intelligence, were nothing but number relationships, and as the numbers that make up the sacred quaternary produce the number ten when they come together (adding together), the number four was considered the most perfect of all due to the same circumstance.

We have already said that the number four represents for the ancient cabalists the four elements: four is, then, the earth, the form; one is the principle of life, the spirit; consequently, *five* is four and one; *five* is, therefore, the spirit dominating the elements, that is, the fifth essence. Thus the pentagram (five-pointed star) manifests that domain. Also the five-pointed pentagram is the number of Jesus, whose name having five letters, is the son of God becoming man, Jehovah incarnate.

It is with the help of the sign of this pentagram that we reproduce here, that the cabalists intend to chain the demons that swarm in the air, the salamanders, the undines and the gnomes.

The pentagram is the flaming star of the Gnostic schools; but it is also, according to whether the spirit is more or less apt to direct matter, good or evil, day or night.

Five is the spirit and its forms.

Black magic uses the pentagram, placing two of its points in the air, which represent the antagonism of good and evil, immobility and ignorance, since the pentagram being thus placed, it is seen that the two horns dominate the ternary, representing the influence of the divine spirit, dominating it.

Five, under these conditions, becomes a fatal number; a bad number placed, according to the Sephirot, under the name of *Geburah*, which is the number of antagonism, autonomy, excessive freedom, and antagonism cannot provoke anything other than rigor.

The pentagram represents the human body, the upper point of which forms the head; if it appears downwards, it is the sign of madness, of imbalance, of inharmony.

The number *six* represents two times *three*: it is, therefore, the image of the relationships that exist between heaven and earth; this is the celestial triangle, of which the terrestrial triangle is the reverse reflection, like that of an object in water; it is the axiom engraved on the Emerald Tablet of Hermes: *what is above is like what is below*; it is the proof of our correspondence with heaven; it is the number of freedom and divine work; freedom is above, work below; it is, consequently, necessary to go through all the steps of the work to reach freedom.

The number *six* is perfect in itself, because the same number results from the addition of its parts.

The septenary is the universal and absolute number, from the point where it contains the quaternary, the ternary, the quinary and the binary.

The number *seven* is sacred in all symbols, because it is composed of the ternary and the quaternary. It represents the magical power in all its force, that is: the spirit assisted by all the elemental powers, it is, like five, the spirit dominating matter; the spirit is not represented by *one*, which means the human spirit, but by three, which represents God, the spirit of God.

If the number *seven* were only in the rainbow, it could be neglected, perhaps rejected; but isn't it everywhere and mainly where the mystery exists? God has placed it in the seven days of creation and has ordered men absolutely to keep and sanctify the seventh day of the week; the number *seven* is in the rainbow, in the musical scale, in the sacraments, in the gifts of the Holy Spirit, in the virtues and in the vices, being the privileged number of poets; fulfilling the apocalypse; it is a mysterious number, and the mystery it contains is of great importance, from the moment God puts it before our eyes, more than seven times a day.

The number *eight*, the *octave*, is: the binary of the quaternary, that is, the universal balance of things, the harmony within the analogy of opposites. The equality of division of *four* has made magicians consider it as the number of justice.

The number *nine*, three times three, is the triangle of the ternary, the most complete image of the three worlds, the basis of all reason, the perfect sense of every verb, the reason for being in all forms. The number nine is that of divine reflections, and manifests the divine idea in all its abstract power.

The number *ten* is called the universal and the complete, marking the full course of life, because there is no further counting from it other than by replication and because it contains in itself all the numbers whereby it explains them by its own multiplication of them.

The figure TEN is composed of the unit that means being, and the zero that represents not being. It thus encloses God and creation, spirit and matter, and is the *ultra* of human intelligence, which counts everything by that number. The problem of the number 10 is a snake climbing a pole, that is, movement and immobility, idea and matter.

After examining the simple numbers, that is, of those that form the unit, we will say that this or that number is linked to the destiny of this or that being, whether at birth, during the course of its life, or at death. There is probably no human being who has failed to notice that this or that date is favorable or unfortunate.[137] Everywhere are the numbers that constitute the dates of even the most insignificant events in life. Numbers divide, subdivide, gather in groups, like light; since there is only one law, they must inevitably follow from the point where they represent harmony.

Each man has, then, his good and his bad numbers, clustering around his favorite groups, in the same way that each artist has his favorite colors or modulations. The numbers or figures that represent them are for men what tones and modes are for painters and musicians, and this being established, we continue our study.

According to Saint Cyprian and Saint Augustine,[138] the number 11 is bad. The law is 10, so 11 is the transgression of the law, that is, sin: it is the number of the rebellion, since it is composed of two columns that represent antagonism, and the strife following the law is rebellion. The number 11 in Cabala

---

137 See otherwise the *Historia de los grandes capitanes*.

138 Translator's note: Saint Augustine (354–430), was a theologian, philosopher, and the bishop of Hippo Regius in Numidia, Roman North Africa.

represents the great magical agent, the hidden and blind force when it is not well directed.

The number 12 is divine, inasmuch as it serves to measure the heavenly bodies, at the same time that it helps the government of the spirits; 12 in Cabala is the number of the philosopher's stone.

Among cabalists, the number 13 does not have the fatal significance that is attributed to it. According to Saint Cyprian, it marks the mystery of the appearance of Jesus Christ to the peoples, because at thirteen days after his birth, he was revealed by the mysterious star that served as a guide to the magi; 13 in *Taurus* represents death, as living beings emerge from the earth: it is rebirth or immortality. The number 13 is that of magical evocations.

The number 14 represents the figure of Jesus Christ, who was slain by the Jews on the fourteenth moon of the first month, and on that day the children of Israel were ordered to celebrate the *phase* to the glory of the Lord, that is, in remembrance or commemoration of the passage of the Red Sea. The 14 in Cabala is regarded as the number of transmutations and metamorphoses, and as a double septenary, it is also regarded as very happy.

15 is a symbol of spiritual ascents, since the 15th day of the seventh month is a day of holiness and rejoicing. However, for cabalists it represents the genius of evil.

16 is a happy number, because it is made up of the dozen and a perfect square.

17 is the number of ill omen, and 18 that of philters and spells, also being that of superstition and error.

In cabala, the number 19 is favorable, because it is composed of 1 and 9, happy numbers that, together, give the perfect 10 par excellence. Nineteen is the number of the sun and that of gold, and also that of the philosopher's stone.

20, cabalistically, is the number of truth, faith and health. The number 21 is as good as the septenary. Three times seven is also the number of divination. The number 22 is good and marks a great fund of wisdom, since 22 are the Hebrew letters and 22 are the books of the Old Testament. The number 22 is the supreme reason in cabala.

28 announces the favor of the moon, because its movement is different from the course of the other stars and it takes place in twenty-eight days.

30 is notable for its many mysteries. Our Lord Jesus Christ was valued at 30 pieces of silver; he was thirty years old when he received baptism, he began to perform miracles and teach the kingdom of God; and John the Baptist was thirty years old when he began preaching in the desert. The Hebrew doctors attributed wisdom to 32, because Abraham, by order of God, opened as many avenues to wisdom. The ancients observe 40, in which they celebrated the festival called *Tessecacosson*;[139] the number 40 is a sign of expiration, of penance and of other mysteries. Moses, Elijah, and Jesus Christ fasted for forty days; the deluge rain lasted forty days; Moses stayed forty days at Sinai; the Israelites forty years in the desert, and Elijah walked forty days without eating to reach the foot of Mount Horeb. Jesus Christ preached publicly for forty days, was hidden forty hours in the tomb, ascended to heaven forty days after his resurrection and instructed his disciples for forty days.

According to Saint Augustine, the number 40 manifests our pilgrimage towards heaven, towards the path of truth. The angels

---

139 Translator's note: This specific reference has not been identified, even on the internet, which is saying something; probably from the Greek τεσσαρακοστός, "fortieth", and perhaps alluding to the forty days between the 1st of Elul and Yom Kippur.

come and go along that path to show us the route and sustain our steps; 40 were also the rungs of Jacob's ladder.

The number 50 means the remission of our sins; it is the number of grace that is attributed to the Holy Spirit.

The number 60 was sacred among the Egyptians, with 72 having a great conformity with 12. Furthermore, the Lord is invoked under 72 names.[140]

The number 100 marks a complete perfection, while 1,000 contains the perfection of all numbers, and is the cube of the denary number, which means absolute perfection.

To finish: simple numbers represent divine things; the tens, celestial things; the hundreds, terrestrial ones, and the thousands, the things of the future.

---

140 Translator's note: Shemhamphorash.

Part Six

THE ETHER

LIFE AND DEATH

Chapter I

The Astral Light

BREATHING is made up of two opposite movements: inhalation and exhalation. These two movements form life, and as soon as they cease it is because life has become extinct.

By the law of harmony that governs all nature, everything breathes in and out here below. Animals also breathe and, like them, all beings placed in a lower degree of creation. The flower, the tree, the plant, breathe in oxygen and breathe out nitrogen, the sea breathes in its ebb and flow, and the earth, our nurse, also breathes. The earth is a man, Hermes Trismegistus has said, and it is through her breathing that she communicates with her children and drags them in that immense chain that unites her with the other worlds of creation. All the breasts, human and celestial, beat with equal movement. The aspiration and expiration of the earth is the astral light, receiving the name of *astral* because the earth is a star. This is the great magic agent. The astral light, which the ancient cabalists have successively called the tetragram, inri, magnetic fluid, serpent, Lucifer, is nothing other than that unknown agent, that latent force that today is called light, heat, electricity, magnetism. This is how they explain the magnetic communications of the earth with the stars.

The sun is the mirage of the reflection of God, and the soul of the earth a permanent gaze of the sun that said earth preserves and keeps by impregnation.

The moon attends this impregnation of the earth, reflecting towards it a solar image (its reflection of it) during the night. And this is why Hermes has said in his *Emerald Tablet*, speaking of the great magical agent: "the sun is its father, the moon is its mother"; adding after this: "the wind has carried it in her womb". For this reason, the atmosphere is the container and like the crucible of the solar rays, through which that living image of the sun is formed, which penetrates the earth completely, vivifies it, fertilizes it and determines everything that is produced on its surface by its effluvia and currents similar to that of the sun itself.

This solar agent lives at the expense of two opposing forces: a force of attraction and a force of projection; whence Hermes says that "it always ascends and descends". It is by this double force that everything has been created and how it subsists.

According to Hermes, from the highest of the heavens the universal spirit is launched without interruption, an inexhaustible source of light and fire, which, passing through all the celestial spheres and finding itself gradually condensed, constantly flows towards the earth. *This is the aspiration.*

Likewise, by the action of the central fire of the sun, continuous emanations rise from the earth which, later sublimated, rise towards the sky to get rid of their impurities. *This is the expiration.*

This eternal and constant rotation of vital molecules is painted in Genesis under the emblem of the mysterious ladder of Jacob and by the ascent and descent of the angels.

Nature, by analogy, reveals this great mystery to us daily. Thus the sun draws in the waters of the swamps and marshes and forms splendid clouds that later become beneficial rain.

Its movement is a successive and indefinite winding and unfolding, or rather, simultaneous and perpetual, by spirals, and of opposite movements that never meet.

It is the same movement as that of the sun that attracts and repels all the stars in its system at the same time. This movement is always double and multiplies in the opposite direction, attractive to the left and repulsive to the right and reciprocally, neither more nor less than the *systolic* and diastolic movements of the human heart.

The stars are chained to each other by networks of light, attractions that keep them in balance and make them move regularly in space; these networks of light go from one sphere to another, without there being a point on each planet to which one of those indestructible threads is not attached.

I already spoke of the human and celestial breasts; now I will deal with those of the stars, because each one of them has its heart and breathes the light like the earth, and like us. Each star has a latent heat and a radiant one. Each star has its centrifugal force, its force of attraction and force of projection and man, as everything is harmony in nature, is in harmony with the stars.

Thus, then, man, like the star, aspires through the heart and the brain, and radiates a fluid around himself, through his voice, through his gestures and through his eyes.

In the center of the earth there is a focus of astral light incessantly maintained by the impregnation of the sun, and that is distributed or dispensed without ceasing to ascend towards the sky. Each star has a central conduit, through which it joins the other stars; man also has a central conduit that connects him with the whirlwinds of light.

The world is magnetized like sunlight, and man is magnetized with astral light. What is operated in the body of the planet is repeated in us. Man is a *microcosm* (a small world), having in him three analogous and hierarchical worlds, as in the rest of nature.

According to the order of analogies, everything that is in the big world (in the macrocosm) is reproduced and produced in the small (microcosm). There are, then, in us three centers of attraction and fluid projection: the brain, the heart or the epigastrium, and the genital organs. Each of these organs attracts on one side and repels on the other. It is through these devices that man communicates with the *universal fluid*, transmitted in him by the nervous system. The brain is in a center of light, and another nervous center is also found in the part of the heart, which is the one that receives the name of *great sympathetic*[141] in cabala.

I have used the word *fluid*, so that it is well understood and because it is the most accurate. Saint Cyprian called it vibration, which is, in his conception, the soul of nature, that is, the breath of God, or the astral light of the *cabalists*.[142]

This force or light is the one that colors the plants, the one that spreads its diamond reflections on the sands of the sea, even within the depths of its bottom; it is the one that lends the magnificent blue to the firmament; it is, in short, life and love.

The four ancient elements, fluids or imponderable vibrations, are nothing but so many manifestations that the ancients knew by the name of quicksilver.

---

141 Translator's note: "gran simpático".

142 In modern natural sciences, the ether is nothing other than that electromagnetic vibration that the ancients knew under that name.

Chapter II

Effects of the Astral Light and the Will

ELECTRICITY is the efficient cause of the excitation of the nerves, the center of which is the brain. Sleepwalkers can, better than in dream, and without losing consciousness of their being, see with the aid of a latent light determined by the electric shock abruptly projected by the magnetizer, the photograph of the places towards which they direct their obedient imagination. And in meditating on this, it should be borne in mind that for electricity there are no distances. This second sight that all beings have, more or less, can also be excited, in the waking state, by the concentration of thought aided by any agent, such as water, fire, or the residue of coffee, inasmuch as something that helps and favors the abstraction of the senses is indispensable.

M. Henry Delaage,[143] imitating Simon the Magician and Saint Cyprian, renewing mystic experiences forgotten, although not lost, and with the help of his will, causes people of a nervous constitution to see clearly, in a glass of water, landscapes, houses, the sacred interior of homes, even when they are located in distant countries. It was enough for him to fascinate them beforehand with his gaze. Making these people concentrate their attention on a single point, he imposed a kind of somnambulism that surpassed the state of vigil, without reaching catalepsy.

Whence the modern proof that there are magnetic relations between human beings and the stars, being more energetic the greater one's nervous irritability.

---

143 Translator's note: Marie Henri Delaage (1825–1882), a French artist/painter.

The somnambulists and the ecstatics enjoy, naturally, the second sight, which is more lucid the more complete the abstraction.

The women who are pregnant are more lucid than those who are not found in that condition, because they are in greater contact with the astral light and the influence that it exerts in the formation of the fetus they carry within them.

Most of the women who are pregnant are subject to strange presentiments, in the same way that they are to strange desires, which the vulgar calls *cravings*. These effects, produced on such an occasion by an exuberance of astral fluid or electricity needed for the formation of the fetus, also occur in extraordinarily nervous people. The sensitive organs have regulated those exuberances.

The men, and among them Apolonio de Tyana,[144] isolated themselves[145] without outside assistance, that is, only by the strength of their will.

Placing their soul in nervous communication with the electricity that encircles the environment in which the being himself moves, they called forth, as if it were a magic mirror, the reflections of existing remote objects and even the reflection of the seeds of the future, being able, in this way, to reveal and predict without reaching the degree of catalepsy, nor even ecstasy.

The astral drunkenness makes the human being insensitive to the things of this world.

But, in another order of things, the will or a powerful concentration of thought produces the same effects. Here is explained the secret of those men, who are admired for their inventiveness and their ingenuity.

---

144 Translator's note: Apollonios of Tyana, a Greek Neopythagorean philosopher of the first century.

145 Currently this act receives the name of auto-suggestion.

The somnambulist is forced, in order to see in the astral light, to abjure his will and serve another. The superior being, by his own will, orders the sidereal body and is served by it as by an instrument, like a slave, to come into direct relationship with that light. In this case he sees, foresees and predicts.[146]

The power of the will can go as far as the will: if you want your body to be filled with scars, like that of Saint Francisco, you need do no more than direct your will towards it; if you want your body to stay long without breath and without feeling, you will get it by your own means, as if yearning to be reduced to the state of the person who has demonstrated the greatest indifference in this life.

From here it is deduced that everything that is desired with true will, sooner or later is achieved.

---

146 Translator's note: "prevé y adivina".

Chapter III

Body And Soul

I HAVE already said that the sidereal body is our instinct, in the same way that our mind is our reason. Instinct, therefore, must be silent when reason speaks, when it watches. The sidereal body is the intermediary between the soul and the material body, and its influence can be great. According to the *Cabala*, the material body gradually takes the form of the animals towards whom our inclinations are most alike, modifying the features of the physiognomy and of the limbs, which produces a kind of similarity with the animals to whom it is alluded. In addition—always according to cabalists—the sidereal body is not in all cases of the same sex as the terrestrial body, having, frequently, a kind of hermaphrodism in us, which means that, when a man lets the influence of petty passions dominate him, he gives up his manhood and becomes truly a woman, by taste, by manners, and even by actions. More than one woman has become a man, sometimes participating in both sexes (hermaphrodism), and this abandonment of her own nature, when it goes to excess, often leads to the most infamous vices. When that hermaphrodism is well directed, exquisite qualities grow in a being; in men it creates poets, makes men frank and generous and self-sacrificing, and in women it grants them the energy necessary for great sacrifices and great virtues.

Material excesses alter the organization of the sidereal body, which, in turn, works sympathetically on the brain and makes it feel the backlash of its wound, whence proceed the nervous diseases, because the material body also suffers, in turn, the faintness of the soul.

A disease always comes from an excess, the origin of a physical evil *always* encountering that of a moral disorder.

The mind is the only thing that distinguishes us from animals, which have, like us, the sidereal body. They can read in the astral light, like sleepwalkers, who are given this faculty, immersing them in a fictitious dream or lethargy through the astral enervation that the magnetizer projects. Animals, like sleepwalkers, divine storms, earth tremors, great cataclysms in nature, and even anticipate supernatural apparitions.

Idiots, who only act by instinct, often receive the gift of second sight, by which they have announced what happened at great distances.[147]

The beings that dedicated their lives to *contemplative instinct*, and in this case were the Chaldean shepherds, possessed a high degree of magical forces, by means of which they were able to subjugate and defeat the Egyptians, who were themselves wisely ruled by the chaste Joseph, who learned the magic of Abraham in his land, being able, for that reason, to explain to Pharaoh the meaning of his dreams, as well as those of his fellow prisoners.

The same can be said of Moses, who, by means of magical forces, was able to liberate the Hebrew people and cross the Red Sea, make water flow in abundance from the stones of the desert to quench the thirst of the Hebrew people, produce the *mana*

---

147 In modern times, Nodier tells us about Francois les bas bleus, who saw what was happening at great distances, and in antiquity the examples that history tells of such gifts are numerous and remarkable. Joan of Arc possessed in the highest degree the gift of enlightenment.

Translator's note: Jean Charles Emmanuel Nodier (1780–1844) was an influential French author and librarian who introduced a younger generation of Romanticists to the *conte fantastique*, gothic literature, and vampire tales. Also, François les bas-bleus is an 1883 *opéra comique* in three acts.

that should feed them, talk with God on Mount Sinai, defeat the enemies that he encountered in his transit and many other wonders that it would be long to list.

Next in Saint Cyprian's narrative, he says that excesses and bad life conclude by chaining the mind to its inactivity, the being then living by nothing more than instinct, which is only secondary, voluntarily placing itself below the zoological scale, whose instinct is not for animals what reason is for us.

These beings are dead before dying; they march and speak even when they are nothing but corpses. They cause cold when they approach their fellow men, and they give you goose bumps when they touch you. They have glassy eyes, a sunken mouth, drooping lips, and swollen eyelids; they will be able to walk around the earth for some time, but without life, without heat.

Such a category of beings form the transition between man and ghost, the sidereal body being that through which beings communicate with the stars, a fact that requires particular details.

Chapter IV

What Is the Human Being and How the Will Is Exercised

IN THIS lower world *everything* is the product of an ethereal substance, the common basis of many phenomena known under the misnomer of *electricity, heat, light, galvanic* and *magnetic* fluid, etc. The universality of the transmutations of this substance constitutes what is commonly called matter.

The brain is the *flask* where the *animal* transports what, depending on the strength of that apparatus, each of its organs can absorb of this substance, and from which *flask* it comes out transformed into will.

The will is a *fluid*, an attribute of every being endowed with movement.

In man, the will becomes a force that is its own and that exceeds in intensity that of all species.

More or less perfect, the innumerable forms that thought affects come from the human apparatus.

The will is exercised by the organs commonly called the *five senses*, which are only one: the FACULTY OF SEEING.

All things that come to be in the domain of the *unique sense*, the *will to see*, are reduced to some elemental bodies whose principles swarm in the air, in the light, or in the principles of air and light. *Sound* is a modification of air; all *colors* are modifications of light; all scent is a combination of *air* and *light*. Thus, the four expressions of matter in relation to man, *sound, color, smell* and *form*, have the same origin. The day is not far off when the affiliation of the principles of light with those of the air is recognized. Thought, which tends to light, is manifested by the word, which tends to sound.

It is already known that in high magic the sound, the color, the scent and the form are lost or reunited in the astral light, of which they are part.

Chapter V

Synergy and Theurgy of the Macrocosm and the Microcosm

CYPRIAN says, Synesius[148] having confirmed it later, that man, like God, contains in himself three persons, namely: the *mind*, the *sidereal body* and the *terrestrial body*. Always the three worlds of the Cabala! The *divine world*, the *abstractive world* and the *instinctive world*. The terrestrial body that serves as matter and that must necessarily return to matter, is driven towards material pleasures, for which reason it tries to seduce and corrupt the MIND by the attraction of sensual pleasures, calling to dominate and guide the body.

It has passions as auxiliaries, above all voluptuousness. The *sidereal* body is thus the intermediary between the soul and the material body and serves as a link with the heart, the source of the life of the body and the brain, the seat of the life of the soul.

The mind, the soul, is the divine spark that lives in us; it is our guide, our conscience, our torch during our stay on earth.

The soul can be kind to the body; it may allow her from time to time to enjoy the pleasures of earthly life, but on condition that she is not made its slave. If the soul is temperate and just, if it loves everything that is beautiful, noble and elevated, humanity, justice, good faith, the country and, above all, loves its neighbor and sublime charity, then when the day of death has come, it leaves the terrestrial envelope and flies according to the planetary

---

148 Translator's note: A Greek bishop of Ptolemais in ancient Libya, a part of the Western Pentapolis of Cyrenaica after the year 410.

attraction and goes back to another universe, where it makes new clothes analogous to the progress of its beauty, leaving, on the one hand, the material corpse on earth, inert in appearance, but already working, by its own decomposition, to attend new creations, and on the other, the *sidereal* corpse, which rises like a luminous mantle, to carry the astral light, in which everything is impregnated, the image, the reflection, the ghost of the body on the earth.

If, on the other hand, the mind allows itself to be subjugated by the gross passions of the body, if it has allowed itself to deceive and lie, crapulous voluptuousness, injustice, everything that is low and bad, then on the day of death, the astral corpse, *strengthened by the condescension of the spirit*, will retain the imprisoned soul—as during its life—, delivering it to the sidereal body, which will drag it in the whirlwinds of the astral light.

Then, according to true magic—and these ideas cannot be admitted without admiring their poetry full of greatness—, the soul, outside its harmonic sphere, will experience cruel tortures and all its energetic tensions will be used in seeking a new covering of flesh, to return to earth and suffer the tests of a second existence, where it can, fighting its previous instincts, which lost it due to their perversity, fly towards the star whose influence particularly dominated in its life. Thus, the mind comes again to imprison itself in a body to begin a new life, but as a *returning soul*.

The first time, as a *new soul*, everything smiled upon him; poetry like the *ops* of the *orphic mysteries*, wealth, nobility, beauty. This time he returns to earth to atone for his past faults, to suffer. He was rich and now he is poor; he was beautiful and now he is ugly; he would continue to have the affliction of sensual pleasures, in which he based his happiness in the other existence, and that now would be a source of temptations that he could not satisfy, monstrous appetites that gnawed at his entrails and would be the twister of his existence. The punishment could not be more appalling: he was the owner and became a slave; he humiliated and is now humiliated; then he was cruel and now he has to suffer. At every step new obstacles arise for him.

If he suffers with courage and resignation, if his soul, tempered by misery, resists his bad instincts, then when he leaves his disgusting wrappings, he regains his glorious path towards the visual star, towards which his aspirations and hopes tend.

But, if he succumbs again, then he will become ill with consumption, idiocy, impotence, etc., etc., condemned from birth to daily physical suffering, then incapable of bad passions, seeing himself one day purified by pain; this is why among the Arabs and the cretins, in the valleys of Switzerland, they are respected as beings touched by the hand of God.

The *mind* must still revive; but then he enters the world with the qualities of *new souls*, and from time to time he will perceive in his judgment something like a vague memory of his past sufferings.

He has, therefore, as a guide, his forebodings and, moreover, a secret horror of the dire inclinations that contributed to his loss. The non-violent nature never leaves man intact his free will, giving him, on the other hand, no other support than reason and the faculty of receiving divine inspirations more energetically, which he will follow willingly, to reach complete regeneration, a faculty which, in theology, is called *grace*. If the soul triumphs then, the tests are over. The divine spark leaves the heavens and to the heavens she must return.

This is how the ancient magicians explained the inequality of character and conditions of human beings, how unjust they seem to us on earth.

Chapter VI

Imagination and Sympathetic Attraction

WHAT is called *imagination* among us is nothing other than the inherent property of our soul to assimilate itself to the images and reflections contained in the *astral light*.

Those forms of the objects that submit to the light are a modification of the light, where the reflection sends them. Thus the astral light, or the terrestrial fluid, which is called the *great magical agent*, is saturated with images or reflections of all kinds, which our soul can evoke, or if you like, call forth its inner sight.

Nothing perishes in nature, and everything that has lived continues to live in new forms; thus, since the previous new forms have not been destroyed, they continue to live and we find them in our memory. Do we not see in our imagination the child that we knew in his childhood turned old? The traces that we considered erased in our memories are not really erased, because a fortuitous circumstance evokes them and reminds us of them. But how do we see them? It has already been said; in the astral light that transmits them to our brain through the mechanism of our nervous apparatus.

Thus—modern magicians say—, all lost science will be found again one day or another, whence the elements that constituted it have been written in the light and are waiting for the sympathetic attraction of an intelligence that is especially devoted to them, to come assimilate them and produce them when the right time has come.

The smell of rain, the murmur of the wind, the roar of the storm, the conjunction of two planets, an eclipse, the sight of the sea, the sound of a bell, the sight of the wheat fields that bend under the weight of their fruit ... they are enough, when awakening the nervous sensitivity of man, whose mission is to reestablish, to awaken in him an idea, already inscribed in the light since other beings thought of it. Being called to carry out that mission, through study, he came to acquire an exquisite sensitivity, his pulse beat more violently than that of others, convolutions of his brain reached greater development and he became a genius.

To hear the voice of God—the ancient magicians said—, who speaks in nature, it is necessary to experience a moment of enthusiastic fever that ennobles the human being, transforming him beyond the spheres of humanity and showing his fellow men one of the leaves of the big book.

"Universal ideas"—said the great Fenelon[149]—"are necessary, eternal, immutable. They are not our ideas, but God's own."

When we keep watch, in our waking state, real objects prevent us from seeing the astral images that obviously surround us, or, if you like, our mind dominates our sidereal body and chains the exercise of its faculties; but when we sleep, the mind rests and the sidereal body comes into relation with those images that we see, often in a vague and incoherent way, but sometimes also true and distinct, especially when a dream has come after a serious concern, or a strong desire.

---

149 Translator's note: François Fénelon (1651–1715) was a French archbishop, theologian and writer.

Chapter VII

Mysteries of Fertilization and Attraction

FOR the initiates, the ether, the soul of the universe, the astral light, is the motive of nature, and this is nothing other than the radiation of God. The forces of the spirit are manifested with the help of a subtle breath that fills the vaults of the brain. Around the nerves there is, then, an invisible atmosphere, the magicians recognizing in the act of generation the breath or *seminal fluid*, that is, the *seminal aura*, which was originally accorded even the power to engender in isolation. The exchange, then, of this seminal fluid, between two beings of different sex, is what produces the fertilization of the human being; in what is well understood, which is from the condensation of that fluid, which by virtue of the will becomes substance, from which the sperm of the father and the seminal liquor of the mother are formed. From the moment that the man's sperm lays the egg in the mother's ovary, the embryonic fetus suffers the influences of the planets and especially the most vehement of a principal one, a fact that is explained by the infinite variety of the human species. By virtue of what mystery are such influences produced?

The answer is simple; that the astral light is composed of different fluids emanating from the seven main stars of our planetary system, in the same way that light is composed of seven rays that have a single point of concentration. Thus, then, human beings attract *more especially*, either by their hereditary conformation or by the time of their birth, the influence of the planet that dominated the sky at that time, receiving its signature as objects receive colors. This being so, however, just as an acid can change one color and replace it with another, be it primitive, be it mixed, so too the will, when it is very vehement, can completely modify and change the native character. The only difference that exists is that while the color is absorbed by a new combination, instead the character is dominated by powerful longings and irresistible impulses. However, despite everything, both color and character will always show reappearing tendencies.

The stars, in their successive movements by constantly extending the network of their fluids, each of which dominates in turn, form the plays of light that give the ether a more or less blue color and more or less gray or ashen, orange, violet or white, at the same time that they contribute to form gloomy clouds and storms.

Once the fetus is fertilized, and already in a position to see the light of day, the being, as it grows, it is clothed with the *sidereal body* first, which is the one that prepares it to receive the soul, that is, to penetrate into the ternary terrain. If the influences of the planet, being a *primitive soul*, are good, that being could overcome those of the fluid that spawned it; but if he is a *returning soul*, he will have no choice but to suffer the inescapable laws that are required for purification, which laws are indicated in another chapter. As regards the corporal beauty of the *terrestrial body*, this must necessarily be in relation to the advance that the *sidereal body* has obtained in previous existences and the divine spark that brings beings closer to the author of creation, that is, the *ethereal soul*.

However, planetary influences can be modified, not only by will, but with the help of talismans. To this end, the complete *Treatise on True Magic or Sorcerer's Treasure*[150] can be consulted, which deals extensively with this matter, and which, as has been said, constitutes the first and main part of this treatise.

---

150 Translator's note: Reference to the *Book of Saint Cyprian*.

Chapter VIII

Man in Relation to the Stars

COMPOSITION OF THE ASTRAL LIGHT OR ELECTRIC FLUID

YOU ASK me, beloved neophytes, why nature grants one person ingenuity, another memory, this one with willpower, that one with talent, another with sagacity,[151] and another with constancy. You would have excused the question if you had meditated that, as all the stars have a direct analogy with terrestrial things, it is said that each human being is born under the influence of a certain planet, the inequality that you think you notice in the work of nature proceeding from this fact. The ancient cabalists divided men, for this reason, into seven well-defined categories, each of which was influenced, more or less vehemently, by a main star, and could also receive secondary influence from other stars.

Thus there are seven main colors, by means of whose mixtures and combinations a complete diversity of tones is obtained, although always preserving the generative harmony. So there are also seven signatures that magicians admit in man, and in the same way as an object, vested mainly in a principal color, does not reflect the others in an absolute way, since this or that circumstance can make them reappear, in the same way, in men (human beings) this or that temperament, this or that trait prevail, be it by their hereditary conformation, or by the time of

---

151 Translator's note: The mental ability to understand and discriminate between relations.

their birth, due to the influence of the planet that dominated in the sky at the time of their aforementioned birth.

The constant study of red magic has led cabalists and magicians to analyze the astral light—of which it has already been spoken—, and to define it as the aspiration and expiration of the universal soul, and as the movement or the incessant light, now making its presence evident by a jolt, now continuing latently a march that never stops. This done, it makes us go a little further, saying that the great electric fluid, the astral light, is composed of different fluids emanating from the seven main stars of which our planetary system is composed, in the same way that light is composed of seven rays that have a single point of concentration.

ORIGIN OF LIGHT AND SOUND

The stars, in their successive movements and by braiding and weaving the network of fluids in which each one dominates in turn, do not, by chance, form the plays of light with which they color the firmament, the gloomy clouds, the calm and the storms. Doesn't a musical harmony result from this perpetual movement, whose divine chords do not reach our obtuse senses, but which perfect beings, the so-called saints, perceive in their ecstasy and who do not listen to it for any other reason than the sublimity of their thoughts? Pythagoras believed so, for which reason painters have placed harps in the hands of angels, just as the pagans placed in those of the god Pan a *seven*-pipe flute.

Sunlight is not exclusively necessary for creation, as is generally thought. Not all flowers open under the influence of solar effluvia,[152] nor do all plants grow thanks to these. The sad tree of the Moluccas only blooms at night.[153]

Each herb grows in the way that suits it. Man is also distinguished by a special shape adapted to his individuality. And just as by the shape of the grass its species is recognized, the character of man is also recognized by its configuration. The study of divine signatures teaches us to give each thing its true name, not to call the wolf a lamb, or a fox the dove, since the true name is written in the very form. Nature has established special characters that form the signature of each member, and with the help of these signatures reveals the most intimate secrets of all human organization, and of man above all. Nothing that exists lacks a particular sign; the only thing that man lacks is to see that sign.

---

152 Translator's note: Effluvia is defined as vapors, invisible particles or auras.

153 Translator's note: The nutmeg tree, *Myristica fragrans*, is a large evergreen tree native to Southeast Asia. Until the late eighteenth century, it only grew in one place in the world: a small group of islands in the Banda Sea, part of the Moluccas—or Spice Islands—in northeastern Indonesia.

Chapter IX

Influence of the Constellations and Planets

ASTRONOMY originated among the Chaldeans, later spreading, first, throughout Egypt, and later throughout the East.

Both the planets and the constellations or houses in which they stop on their way through space have an analogy with terrestrial things and give us an indication, knowing how to find their constellations, of the most hidden things. They predict to man his evils and miseries, influence the course of his life, make him sick or cure him; in a word, they exert a powerful influence on all actions in his life.

The seven planets are: *Sun, Moon, Venus, Mars, Jupiter, Mercury* and *Saturn*. The Sun presides over the head; the Moon, the right arm; Venus, the left; Jupiter, the stomach; Mars, the sexual parts; Mercury, the right foot, and Saturn, the left.

The constellations rule: *Aries*, the head; *Taurus*, the neck; *Gemini*, arms and backs; *Cancer*, the breast and the heart; *Leo*, the stomach; *Virgo*, the belly; *Libra*, the kidneys and buttocks; *Scorpio*, the sexual parts; *Sagittarius*, the thighs; *Capricorn*, the knees; *Aquarius*, the legs, and *Pisces*, the feet (See the engraving on the next page, which was also published in a work of medicine, of 1495, and whose drawing is a graphic demonstration of the above).

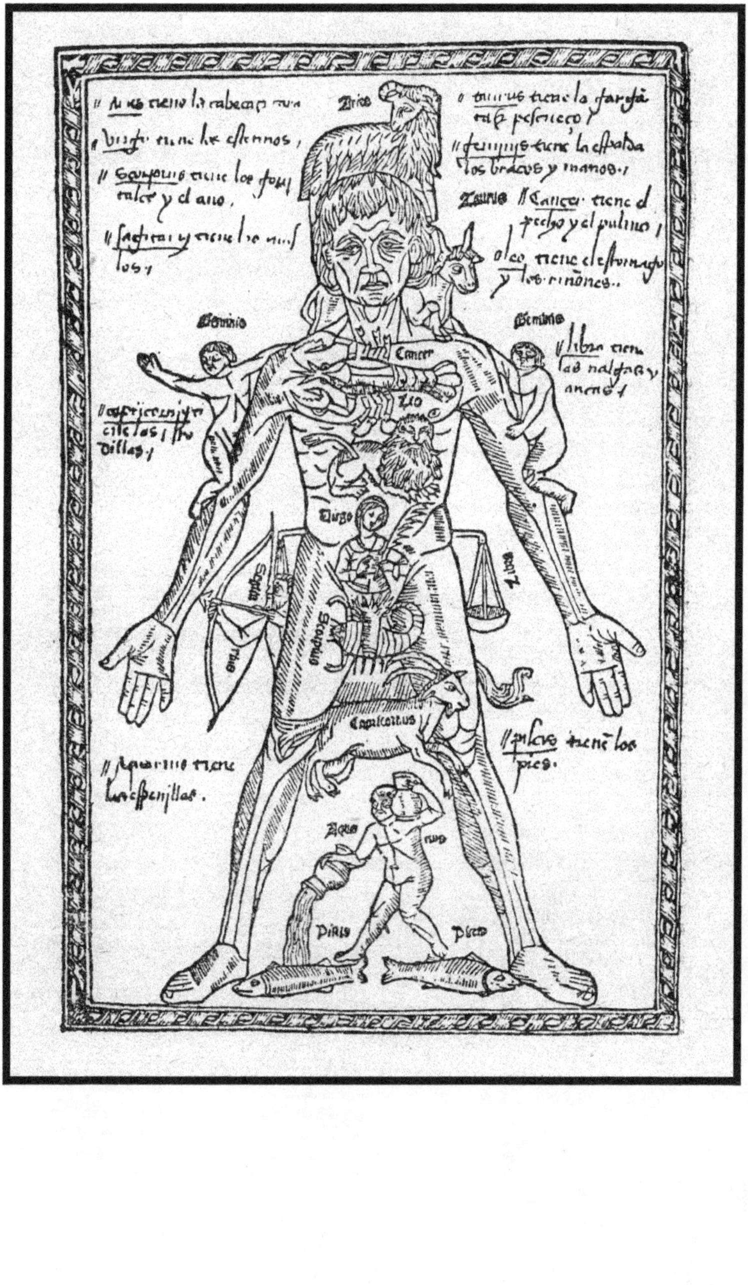

Aries
Taurus
Geminis
Cancer
Leo
Virgo
Libra
Scorpius
Capricornus
Pisces

They also preside over the seven holes of the head, in the following way: *Saturn* and *Jupiter*, the two ears; Mars and *Venus*, the two nostrils; the *Sun* and the *Moon*, the two eyes, and *Mercury*, the mouth.

Each of the signs of the Zodiac occupies a place called a *celestial house of the Sun*, whose twelve houses also cut the Zodiac into twelve parts, each of which occupies 30° (degrees). Hence the twelve months of the year and the 28, 29, 30, or 31 days of each month, the time that the Sun remains in each of those twelve houses.

Aries is the first house, which is also called the *eastern angle*. It is the house of life, and those who are born when this constellation dominates can live a long time.

Taurus, which is called the *inner door*, is the house of riches and treasures, where the means of fortune reign.

The third is that of *Gemini*, also called the *room of the brothers*, and is the house of inheritances and high positions.

The fourth is that of *Cancer*, called the *bottom of the sky, the corner of the earth, the home of the relatives*, and it is the house of treasures and patrimonial goods.

The fifth is that of *Leo*, or *abode of the children*, and it is the house of bequests and donations.

The sixth is that of *Virgo*, called the *love of Mars*, and is the home of sorrows, misfortunes and diseases.

The seventh, that of *Libra*, called the *western angle*, is the house of marriages and weddings.

The eighth is that of *Scorpio*, called the *upper gate*; it is the house of terrors, fears and death.

The ninth, that of *Sagittarius*, called *love of the sun*, is a house of piety, religion, travel and philosophy.

The tenth, that of *Capricorn*, is also called the *center of heaven*, and is the house of high positions, jobs, dignities, etc.

The eleventh, that of *Aquarius*, called the *love of Jupiter*, is the home of friends and wealth.

Finally, the twelfth, that of *Pisces*, called the *love of Saturn*, is the worst and most fatal of all; it is a house of poisonings, miseries, envy, bad characters and violent death.

The favorite houses of *Mars* are those of *Aries* and *Scorpio*; those of *Venus, Taurus* and *Libra*; those of *Mercury, Gemini* and *Virgo*; those of *Jupiter, Sagittarius* and *Pisces*; that of the *Sun, Leo*, and that of the *Moon, Cancer*.

It is no longer convenient, but necessary, to carefully examine the encounters of the planets with the constellations. If, for example, *Mars* meets *Aries* at birth, it infuses, being born under that influence, courage, pride and long life. If with *Taurus*, wealth and value; in a word: *Mars* increases the influence of the constellations it meets, adding courage and strength to them.

Saturn, which brings with it sorrows, miseries, and illnesses, increases bad influences and destroys good ones. *Venus*, on the contrary, increases the good influences and weakens the bad ones, giving, as has already been said, loves and pleasures.

Mercury increases or weakens the influences, according to its conjunctions; for example, if it meets Pisces, which is bad, and if it meets *Capricorn*, which is conducive, the influence will be better.

The *Moon* adds melancholy to happy constellations, sadness or madness to misfortunes; *Jupiter*, who gives riches and at the same time honors, increases good influences and diminishes bad ones. The *Sun* in its ascent, grants favors and has almost as much effect on influences as *Jupiter*; but descending heralds misfortune.

To what has been said it must be added that *Gemini, Libra* and *Virgo* grant beauty par excellence; *Scorpio* and *Pisces*, a certain fairness that does not reach beauty, while the other constellations can only cause ugliness, more or less attenuated by the direct influence of the planet.

Virgo, Libra, Aquarius and *Gemini* give a beautiful voice, and *Cancer, Scorpio* and *Pisces*, a very ungrateful timbre; the other constellations have no influence on the glottis.

If the planets and constellations are in your east at the time of the horoscope, you will feel their influence at the beginning of life or what you want to undertake; it will be tested in the middle, if they are high in the sky, and at the end of life or the matter being consulted if they already fall in the west.

Among the constellations, *Aries, Leo* and *Sagittarius* are warm, dry and light; *Taurus, Virgo* and *Capricorn*, heavy, cold and dry; *Gemini, Libra* and *Aquarius*, either light, warm and humid, or mild and cold.

Every day of every hour of the week is under the influence of a planet. Sometimes there are double influences, which can be combined or destroyed. The hours are counted from noon to noon the next.

It must be taken into account that a planet is in conjunction with another when it passes in front of it; thus, when there is an eclipse of the Sun, there is a conjunction between the Moon and the Sun, and when Venus passes in front of the disk of the Sun, there is a conjunction between both planets, and so on.

The conjunction and opposition of the stars are called *signs*.[154] The stars are in conjunction, opposition or square, with respect to the Sun; but also a planet is in conjunction, opposition or square with respect to another planet, according to the difference between their longitudes. When a star is in a square, its distance from the Sun will differ by three or four signs.

---

154 Translator's note: "signos"; more commonly known as *aspects* in modern astrological terminology.

PREVENTIONS

The condensation of the atmosphere that forms those dense and opaque veils that are called *clouds*, also exerts a great influence on all our investigations and desires. Thus, when trying to compose philters or consecrate talismans, the operation cannot be done as long as those veils cover the firmament, or, at least, diminish the brightness of the star to whom the operation is consecrated or whose influence is desired, since neither the one nor the other would have an effect.

Chapter X

How to Make the Horoscope

THE CONJUNCTION and opposition of the stars are called signs. These are in conjunction, opposition or square, with respect to the Sun; but also a planet is in opposition, conjunction or square with respect to another planet, according to their different longitudes.

When a star is in a square, its distance from the Sun will differ by three or four signs.

The apparent motion of the planets and satellites, observed from Earth, is the result of a great combination of their particular motions. For this reason, sometimes, a planet is *stationary*, this happening because it does not increase or decrease in longitude. If it is at all backward when it moves in the direction of its effective movement, it is *retrograde*, decreasing in longitude. When it moves in the direction of its effective movement increasing its longitude, it is *direct*.

The observations made from the Sun are called *heliocentric*, and from the center of the Earth, *geocentric*. The former are used to calculate the places of the planets, satellites, constellations, etc., and the observations here on Earth, for the cure of diseases, discoveries of mines and collection of plants.

To present the movements of all planets and satellites, according to their true direction, the following observations should be carefully considered.

If you imagine an observer positioned with his head towards the North Pole and his feet towards the South Pole of the equinoctial, the rotary motion of the Earth and the translation of the Moon will be from right to left. In this same sense, the

Earth and the planets move around the Sun, with respect to an observer placed in said star.

If an observer imagines himself placed in the same terms on any planet, the movement of his satellites will be in the same way. But if the position of the observer is inverse, that is, if his head is the one that corresponds to the South Pole and his feet to the North Pole, the movements expressed will be made to the right.

These opaque and dense veils that sometimes cover all the stars, which we call clouds, also exert a great influence on all our investigations. For this reason, no philters should be composed or talismans made, as long as those veils cover the influence of the stars, because everything that is done would not produce any effect.

"For my precise observations"—says Abraham Zacutti[155] himself—, "I stop the storms with my influence, and my magic power is so much, that I return nature to its primitive state. Identify yourselves with me, do not lose heart, and the whole of nature will obey you."

This being established, now see the method and means that you have to put into practice to be able to find a horoscope or the object that is needed.

In order for the horoscope not to be wrong, it is necessary to start operations *precisely* at the minute the being was born, a boy or a girl, or at the critical moment when you are going to start an undertaking whose consequences you want to foresee in advance. Suppose, then, that you want to find or know the celestial influence of a child who has just been born.

---

155 Translator's note: Abraham Zacuto (1452–1515) was a Spanish astronomer, astrologer, mathematician, rabbi and historian who served as Royal Astronomer to King John II of Portugal, prince of astrologers and author of the best astronomical tables that have been published, including those of Alfonso the Wise, or el Sabio (1221–1284), king of Castile and Leon from 1252 to 1284.

Let us suppose that the child is of the male sex and that he was born on *Wednesday, March 5, 1902, at six in the morning.* I take the astrolabe and find that he was born in the sign of *Pisces,* number 12 from the house of the Sun.

He was born, then, on *Wednesday,* the day of the planet *Mercury,* which has the number 10, for which I write in the box where he was born, that is, 12; then I do the same with the other planets, leaving the 1, 3, 5, 7 and 9 empty.

He was born at six in the morning, when Jupiter predominates in the sky. I then go to Jupiter, to number 12, and I throw a dash below to indicate that it is the time the child was born. Once this is done, one must look for which conjunctions the sun is found in on Wednesday, March 5, for which I take a map of the planisphere, or of the spheres, that is very exact, and I find myself a rule. I look for the box of Pisces in its northern hemisphere; I find it ruling the March and April. I look in the previous circle for March 5, and when I have found it, I throw a line from March 5 to the Arctic Pole. The constellations and stars that are below that line will be precisely those that on that day were found in conjunction with the Sun. I take note and transfer them to the boxes that I have left empty in my astrolabe, and the horoscope will be made as follows:

The child is in the sign of Pisces, a house of misery, envy, resentment and bad humor, and as this sign dominates the hair and head, therefore, it is foretold: that he will suffer a fall from a horse that could be fatal, that he is liable to go to jail and that his life will generally be sad and miserable.

But since the child was born on the 5th of the month, Aquarius will have some influence, and thus it can be predicted that he will have a friend who will favor him and console him in his sadness and affliction. However, his planet is Mercury, as it is known that he was born on Wednesday. As this planet presides over the mouth, the hands, the legs and the imagination, the horoscope is somewhat modified, without this preventing the previous conclusions, to which the following must now be added by virtue of the influence of Mercury; the child will be talkative and express himself very well, he will be a great walker and will have a prodigious memory. Then his hair will be brown, a mixture of blonde and black. His fatal hours were at one and eight in the morning and at three and ten at night. He loves commerce and travel, and particularly he will dedicate Wednesdays completely to commercial tasks.

Now, following the horoscope, as the child was born at five in the morning, the time when Jupiter presides, who dominates destinies, dignities, jobs, this modifies the horoscope again, and the child will not fall from the horse, but will suffer from indigestion, which will take him to the grave at a premature age. A great character will be interested in his fate.

In the same way, one will proceed with respect to investigating the means of finding hidden treasures, inheritances that may ensue, and mines. To this end, one will go to find the planet Jupiter, which is the one that indicates wealth. As the day he reigns is Thursday and his favorite houses are Sagittarius and Pisces, the operation will be executed during the transit of the planet that concerns us to the next one, which is Venus, very beneficial, who rules on Friday, and whose favorite houses are Taurus and Libra, and the combination will be made, but keeping in mind that the sky must be clear, that no small cloud obscures it, having directed the astrolabe over the point where the treasures are sought, to be able to form the proper signs, to see if the star is in square, which will be executed at eleven hours at night, which is the transit of one star to another, warning that the time has to be taken correctly, because the operation, if it were wrong, would not go well.

This is the entire celestial book that has served me in all my operations and that I have consulted countless times, and which is for me the general rule for the other predictions, having always followed the precise instructions of the famous astrologers Leon the Hebrew, Hermes, Berlas, Plinio, Diogenes, and many others that I have studied carefully and whose experiments, carried out according to their indications, have never failed me.

Chapter XI

Mysteries of Virginity and Virgin Blood

THE MAGICAL tradition of all ages accords to virginity a supernatural and divine charm. The prophetic inspirations seek virgins, and it is in hatred of innocence and virginity that *Goetia*[156] sacrifices the girls in whom it recognizes a sacred and expiatory virtue. The fire of the vestals[157] was nothing other than the symbol of faith and chaste love, being also the universal agent that Numa[158] knew how to produce, directing it in an electric and explosive way.

Indeed: to light the fire of the vestals, if by a punishable negligence they had allowed it to extinguish, either the light of the sun or the fire of a lightning bolt was necessary. The blood that the woman consecrates to the man when she gives him her virginity is the most noble that has existed, not only among the Magi, but also among the ancient Romans. Ceasing to love the one to whom the virginal flower has been given is the greatest misfortune that can afflict the heart of a woman, and declaring

---

156 False magic.

————

Translator's note: "Goecia".

157 Translator's note: The fire of Vesta was a sacred eternal flame in ancient Rome. The Vestal Virgins, originally numbering two, later four and eventually six, were selected by lot and served for thirty years, tending the holy fire and performing other rituals connected to domestic life—among them were the ritual sweeping of the temple on June 15 and the preparation of food for certain festivals.

158 Translator's note: Possibly Numa Pompilius, the legendary second king of Rome, to whom the institution of the Vestals was attributed.

that surrender aloud is something like denying past innocence and renouncing the honesty of the heart, and the integrity of honor, which constitutes the last and most irreparable of all shames. Among magicians, when marriage is no longer sacred, decadence or perversion and punishment do not wait.

Nobody, however, is perfect in this lower world, for which I want to show you some of the mysteries that the virginal blood contains. In the first place, the woman who thinks something of herself and contemplates the future, will have to keep the shirt with which she went to the nuptial bed to make the sacrifice of her virginity to the beloved man. That shirt, impregnated with blood, will have the virtue of attracting him on the day he goes astray, the day he begins to be adulterous and impure. Placing the shirt under the pillow of the alleged adulterer, she will have the virtue of attracting him to the right path and making him forget the affection that other women could give him or that other women had given him.

As far as *non-virginal* blood is concerned, a single drop that a woman spills during her menstrual period, mixed with any food or drink, is enough for the woman who shed it to win the love of the man she loves, or retain the one who for any circumstance would like to get away from it.

Chapter XII

Fluid Larvae and Elemental Spirits

IMPERFECT OR EARTHLY SPIRITS

THE FLUIDIC larvae are nothing other than the elemental spirits that surround every human being and have a body of air formed by the vapors of blood. That is why they seek blood that is spilled, when they are not nourished by the smoke that is given off from sacrifices.

How were these larvae formed?

The magical tradition maintains that they are the children of Adam's loneliness, born of his dreams when he aspired to the woman who had not yet been granted by the Lord.[159]

When they are condensed enough to be seen, they are nothing more than a vapor colored by the reflection of an image. They do not have a life of their own, but they imitate the life of those who form or evoke them, as the shadow imitates the body.

They occur especially around people who are idiots or who indulge in solitary or immoral acts. Hence the fact that all magicians have condemned those who indulge in solitary pleasures.

These larvae are also formed as a result of the four humors, namely: blood, which corresponds to air; choler, which comes from fire; phlegm, coming from water, and melancholy, originating from the earth. These humors agree with the four seasons of the year, the blood corresponding to spring; the choler,

---

159 Paracelsus affirms and maintains that the blood lost, either regularly, or in dreams for celibate beings of either sex, populated the air with phantasms.

to the summer; melancholy, to autumn, and phlegm, to winter.

The cohesion of the parts of their fantastic body is very weak, for which they fear strong air, fire and the point and cutting edge of any sharp weapon.

They become a kind of vaporous appendix to the real body of their parents, since they do not actually live without the lives of those who have created them or who appropriate them by evoking them.

These larvae attract towards themselves the vital heat of healthy people and quickly exhaust the forces of those who are weak, either by temperament or by premature expiration.

Hence the stories or legends of vampires; unfortunately real and periodically verified stories.

This is why when *mediums* approach, that is, people obsessed with larvae, a general cooling is felt in the atmosphere.

These larvae owe their existence only to the lies of exalted imaginations and to the morbid disorder of beings who indulge in sensual pleasures, particularly masturbation, pederasty, or, if they are women, sapphic love, not occurring in the presence of a person who knows and can tear the veil that covers its origin, and reveal the mystery of its source.

With regard to imperfect spirits, also called earthly or extracorporeal, that is another matter. They were true souls who, having failed to shed the heavy burden of their mistakes, await a new reincarnation; but until that day arrives, the ones who manage to influence those who swarm upon the world, make this humanity, as selfish as it is ignorant, march forever blindly along the paths of life. Only the most spiritual, whom the Catholic religion calls saints, manage to evade these natural laws and even, if you like, physical ones; laws that produced, among the sages of ancient ages and among the Greek philosophers, the negation of free will.

Man feels within himself a force that drives him, that pushes him, that drags him, and that force, or, if you like, call it the aspiration to achieve what is not possessed, pushes him—let us repeat the phrase—, in a manner so fatal, that it goes to heroism or glory, or to ruin and shame. Let's see if it is not so; when man goes after wealth, the richer he is, the more he is eager to possess. When he aspires to glory, all of the known world is insufficient for him. By professing love, he wants to enjoy it at all, without an indiscreet or greedy look, or a lustful desire robbing him of a minimum part.

Why is all this happening? Man suffers, in the first place, from planetary influences; in the second, those of his own complexion, and in the third, the influences of those spirits to which we have referred, which push the matter of living beings, in order to act as if they were also alive, being they who according to the special laws by which they are governed, feel aspirations that they never see satisfied, and they push the fragile matter, so that it leans in the direction that they trace for it. Thus, as has already been said in the course of this work, the idea of yesterday is in fact that of today, and the invention of the day is nothing other than the development of an idea already matured, and that, by the innumerable laws of the nature, remains inscribed in the astral light.

This is why man has yearnings, desires and aspirations, which could even be described as insatiable. And this happens because the spirits that feel imprisoned in matter try to escape it, to fly to other planets, from which fact it can be affirmed that all the misfortunes that humanity suffers (wars, crimes, suicides, diseases, etc.), recognize no other object than the desire of the spirits, which seek to free themselves from the burden that overwhelms them, that is, from the human body, for which they make man proceed in the sense that suits them.

Chapter XIII

Why Did Simon the Magician Fly and How People Can Fly

THE MAGICAL power extends very far; only the magnetic fluid can strike like lightning at a person. But that's not the point: as Simon the magician flew and magnetized and did wonders judged to be supernatural, I have flown and magnetized myself, and any Karcist can do it,[160] and this without appealing to prayers or spells.[161] That power is given by the astral light, which produces electricity up to lightning.

What does it take to acquire that strength? Zoroaster[162] says thus: "It is necessary to know the mysterious laws of balance, which unite the empire of good with the power of evil; it is necessary to have purified the body by the holy tests; having fought against the phantasms of hallucination; having tamed the fantastic monsters that appear to us in dreams; it is necessary, in a word, to use the energetic expression of the oracle, to have heard the light speak."

Solomon has said it also: The will of the human being is powerful, almost omnipotent, when it arms itself with the living energies that nature puts at its disposal.

---

160 Person initiated in the practices of high magic.

161 In the book of which this is an appendix is explained how this experiment is done.

162 Translator's note: Zoroaster, also known as Zarathustra, Zarathushtra Spitama or Ashu Zarathushtra, was an ancient Iranian prophet and founder of Zoroastrianism.

Crisis or ecstasy[163] produces extraordinary effects on the human body.

There is a mixed agent, a natural, bodily and spiritual agent; a common receptacle of the vibrations of movement and of the images of form; a fluid and a force that could be called the imagination of nature. By that force all the nervous apparatus secretly communicates the whole and that universal agent of the works of nature is the Od of the Hebrews.[164]

The existence and possible use of that force are still the great arcanum of practical magic. It is the wand of the thaumaturges and the clavicle of black magic.

It is the Edenic serpent who transmitted to Eve the seductions of the fallen angel.

It is, finally, a blind force in itself, but it is directed by the *egregors*,[165] that is, by the chiefs of the souls. These are the spirits of strength and action. Simon was one while he kept himself pure.

In summary: the astral light, magnetized and clarified magnetism, is a force that attracts, rejects, vivifies, destroys, coagulates, separates, breaks, gathers and elevates under the impulse of strong and powerful wills.

---

163 Ecstasy can exalt the forces of the sidereal body, to the point of making the material body halt in its thrust, which proves that the destiny of the soul is to rise.

164 And the astral light of the Martinists.

Translator's note: Martinism is a form of Christian mysticism and esoteric Christianity concerned with the fall of the first man, his state of material privation from his divine source, and the process of his return, called 'Reintegration' or illumination.

165 Translator's note: Egregore—also spelled egregor; from French égrégore, from Ancient Greek egrégoros, "wakeful"—is an occult concept representing a distinct non-physical entity that arises from a collective group of people.

The magicians of the Pharaohs at first performed the same wonders as Moses, which proves that the instruments were the same. Later the powerful will of the great Hebrew leader overshadowed these magicians.

Chapter XIV

How and Why is Magical Power Lost?

THE SECRETS OF SIMON "THE MAGICIAN" REVEALED BY
SAINT CYPRIAN

THE GERMAN monk Jonas Sufurino says that Saint Cyprian dedicates several chapters of one of his works to examining the life and deeds of Simon the Magician (contemporary, as is known, of our Lord Jesus Christ) under two different aspects, namely: as a thaumaturge and as a true magician.

"Simon"—writes the Saint—"was a Jew by origin, having been born in Gitton, a small town in Samaria. From a very young age he learned the magical sciences from a thaumaturge, more than a magician, called Dossithee,[166] who said he was sent by God and by the Messiah announced by the prophets. From him Simon learned not only the art of magic, but also certain natural arcana, which really belong to the secret tradition of high magic. From the list of acts attributed to him by his contemporaries, it turns out that Simon possessed the science of astral fire and attracted great currents of this fire around him, which made him appear with two of the main qualities that glorious bodies possess, that is, with *impassivity* and *incombustibility*. He also possessed the power to rise and stay in the air; he remotely magnetized those who believed in him and appeared to them in various forms. He

---

166 Translator's note: Another reference of which little is known; although the name of Dositheus is often coupled with that of Simon Magus as the first of all heretics, there is little information to be found concerning him.

produced visible images and reflections, to the point of making fantastic trees and exuberant vegetation appear in the middle of a sterile field or wasteland.[167]

"Naturally inanimate things moved around him, and often, when he wanted to enter or leave a house, the doors creaked and shook before him, eventually opening."

"Thus far"—Saint Cyprian writes verbatim—, "only the magician is seen who, through the Cabala and the clavicle, performs all the wonders that the human being can perform through high magic. In addition"—continues the Saint—, "Simon was endowed with such an extremely impressionable nature that, without having to resort to magic, through ecstasy, excitement and increase of the astral fire that serves as an atmosphere to every human being, he provoked in himself the most extraordinary phenomena. Only in this way can it be explained that as soon as he was seen to be pale, withered and decayed, like an old decrepit man, and about to leave existence, how he was admired for possession of luminous fluids that made his eyes shine, granting him then another of the qualities of the glorious bodies, that of *transparency*, and which softened, at the same time, the features of his physiognomy, which appeared, on those occasions, rejuvenated and revived."

But it happened that, Simon being delighted by the miracles performed by Jesus's disciples and not content with the magical power he possessed, he became corrupted and gave himself up to vice with a slave named Helena, and the magician became a thaumaturge, pretending nothing less than to obscure the

---

167 These same phenomena that psychiatry studies at present, in order to give an account at the International Psychological Congress that should be held in Paris as a result of the foundation in 1900 of the Psychological Institute (rue Serpente, 24), in 1904, they were carried out in our day by the Scottish M. Home and they are still carried out by all people endowed with a great force of attraction and magnetism.

doctrines of Christianity with new ones, the product of his sick imagination. He was exalted in such a way by the passion he conceived for the slave Helena, that he invented a new mythology with magical reminiscences. According to that mythology, the first manifestation of God was a perfect splendor that immediately produced its own reflection. He, Simon the magician, was the sun of souls, and his slave Helena—whom he called *Selena*, a name that in Greek means the moon—, his reflection. Simon's moon descended to earth at the beginning of the ages and she became a mother, because the thought of the sun made her fertile, and she gave birth to angels, whom she cared for and educated by herself without speaking of her father; but the angels rose up and chained her to her mortal body. Then the splendor of God was forced to descend from the heavens, and he who was, came to earth to defeat death, rescued his Selena and took her to heaven through the air followed by a triumphal chariot, in which his elected followers also would go. The rest of the men would be abandoned on earth to the tyranny of the rebel angels.

As of this date, the credit that Simon acquired as a magician was weakening, and although transferred to Rome in 41 AD, he performed some prodigies before the court of Nero; in a public dispute that he had with Saint Peter, when trying to practice the well-known experiments of his flight, he fell and broke his leg, for which he was ashamed and committed suicide by throwing himself out of a window of the house where he lived.

Why did Simon the wizard lose his magic power? Because high magic is reserved for men who are masters of their passions; because the spirit puts on material garments to descend, just as he strips them off to go up.

Because high magic is the absolute science of balance.

Because it is essentially religious, since it has presided over the formation of the dogmas of the ancient world, and has been the mother, if not the nurse, of all civilizations and all sciences.

Before placing the *finis coronat opus*[168] of the ancients on the last page of this treatise, we must make some considerations regarding the end of magic, and particularly of the SUPREME, which is what puts us in contact with God and with the super-spirits.[169]

There is no doubt that all progress is due to the study and investigation of nature, aided by the inspiration of higher spirits and by the true knowledge and application of magic. Thus, religion and progress march together and compact, because they emanate from the same source: from God, who is the Supreme Maker of everything. The magician, then, does not march against God, as is erroneously supposed, but in search of God, with the desire to investigate the supernatural, in order to realize his arcana.

Man cannot offend God with his acts, because God is far superior to man, to the extent that man cannot reach Him except after an uninterrupted series of transformations and successive material lives. The man who insults God does so at the suggestion of perverse and proud spirits, and the man who acts with righteousness and nobility, does so driven by good spirits. All these acts are permitted by God to delay or hasten the hour in which man achieves the supreme perfection to which he marches, and which the translator and commentator of this treatise wishes for all his readers.

---

168 Translator's note: Latin, "the end crowns the work".
169 Translator's note: "superespiritus".

Appendix

Translator's note from page 7:

"This pantheistic image represents Religion or Truth, terrible for the profane and gentle for initiates. It has more than one analogy with the Cherub of Ezekiel. The human figure is placed between a bridled bull and a tiger, thus forming the triangle of Kethar, Geburah, and Gedulah, or Chesed. In the Indian symbol, the four magical signs of the Tarot are found in the four hands of Addha-Nari—on the side of the initiate and of mercy are the sceptre and the cup; on the side of the profane, represented by the tiger, are the sword and the circle, which latter may become either the ring of a chain or an iron collar. On the side of the initiate, the goddess is clothed only with the skin of the tiger; on that of the tiger itself she wears a long star-spangled robe, and even her hair is veiled. A fountain of milk springs from her forehead, falls on the side of the initiate, and about Addha-Nari and the two animals it forms a magic circle, enclosing them in an island which represents the world. The goddess wears round her neck a magic chain, formed of iron links on the side of the profane and of intelligent heads on that of the initiate; she bears on her forehead the figure of the lingam, and on either side of her are three superposed lines which represent the equilibrium of the triad, and recall the trigrams of Fo-Hi." –Eliphas Levi, *Transcendental Magic: Its Doctrine and Ritual* (translation by Arthur Edward Waite), George Redway Publications, 1896.

Translator's note 29:

Spelling mistakes in the original Latin text have been retained. The prayer is printed in the original text without translation, which is provided here:

Most merciful God, whose power has no end, who forever possesses supreme dominion over all your creatures and their affairs, so that nothing can be taken from your empire even by apostasy; we have sinned against you, and will provoke your most just wrath, when we do not obey your commandments, and then most of all, when fleeing from your friendship and lordship, we will deny you and consort with ungodly demons; and since it would not be enough to deny you, we bind ourselves to demons even by writing, and we have handed over that charter of obligation to them to be secured against you. But most merciful Lord, because your mercies are without number, and compassion and forgiveness are always yours; this creature of yours, who denied you and handed over to the demons a charter binding himself, by your infinite goodness may it be returned to him, may he denounce his impiety, and goaded by fear of you, having turned upward and away from the demon, rather be subject to you his Lord, and with a contrite heart desire to receive your grace. We know, Lord, that you will never despise a contrite and humble heart, nor can that charter put in place any obstacle to your mercy, therefore we beg of you on bended knees, that from your abundant pity you not only remit this one's sinful impiety by the blood of your Son our Lord Jesus Christ, but also compel the demons to return the charter of his obligation and submission by presenting your virtuous word; lest he should glory in his own tyranny, or lay claim to any right in the man, whom we pray to be freed from the bonds of his sins by your Son. Through him our Lord Jesus Christ your Son. Amen.)

Translator's note from page 48:

A Jewish chief of the priests at Ephesus (Acts 19:13–16); i.e., the head of one of the twenty-four courses of the house of Levi. He had seven sons, who "took upon them to call over them which had evil spirits the name of the Lord Jesus", in imitation of Paul. They tried their method of exorcism on a fierce demoniac, and failed.

Translator's note from page 74:

Le Veritable Dragon Noir Ou les Forces Infernales, Editions Unicursal, 2017: 94.

Vous volerez un chat noir, et acheterez un pot neuf, un miroir, un briquet, une pierre d'agate, du charbon et de l'amadou, observant d'aller prendre de l'eau, au coup de minuit, a une fontaine. Apres quoi, vous allumez votre feu; mettez le chat dans le pot et tenez le couvert de la main gauche sans jamais bouger, ni regarder derriere vous, quelque bruit que vous entendiez. Apres l'avoir fait bouillir vingt-quatre heures, vous le mettez dans un plat neuf; prenez la viande et la jetez par-dessus l'epaule gauche, en disant: 'Accipe quod tibi do, et nihil amplius.'

Puis, vous mettrez les os, un a un, sous les dents du cote gauche, en vous regardant dans le miroir; et si ce n'est pas le bon, vous le jetterez de meme, en disant les memes paroles jusqu'a ce que vous l'ayez trouve; et sitot que vous ne vous verrez plus dans le miroir, retirez-vous a reculons en disant: 'Pater in manus tuas commendo spiritum meum.'

Conservez cet os, hors de la vue de tout profane; par la suite, il vous suffira de le mettre entre les dents pour vous rendre invisible.

Translation: You will steal a black cat, and buy a new pot, a mirror, a lighter, an agate stone, some charcoal and some tinder, seeing that you take water, at the stroke of midnight, from a fountain. After which, you light your fire; put the cat in the pot and hold the lid with your left hand without ever moving or looking behind you, no matter what noise you hear. After boiling it for twenty-four hours, you put it in a new dish; take the meat and throw it over the left shoulder, saying: 'Accipe quod tibi do, et nihil amplius.'

Then, you will put the bones, one by one, under the teeth on the left side, looking at yourself in the mirror; and if it is not the right one, you will throw it away as well, saying the same words until you find it; and as soon as you no longer see yourself in the mirror, step back and say: 'Pater in manus tuas commendo spiritum meum.'

Keep this bone out of the sight of any layman; then, you just have to put it between your teeth to make yourself invisible.

Bibliography

Agrippa, Henry Cornelius (attributed), *The Fourth Book of Occult Philosophy*, ed. by Stephen Skinner, trans. by Robert Turner (Lake Worth, FL: Ibis Press, 2005)

Agrippa, Henry Cornelius, *Three Books of Occult Philosophy*, ed. by Donald Tyson (Woodbury, MN: Llewelyn Publications, 2019)

Cecchetelli, Michael, *Crossed Keys* (London: Scarlet Imprint, 2011)

Davies, Owen, *Grimoires: A History of Magic Books* (Oxford: Oxford University Press, 2009)

de Abano, Peter (attributed), *Heptameron: or, Magical Elements of Peter de Abano*, trans. by Robert Turner (Seattle, WA: Ouroboros Press, 2003)

Grego, Iroé, *True Black Magic (La véritable magie noire)*, trans. by Joseph Peterson (CreateSpace Independent Publishing Platform, 2017)

Harms, Daniel, James Clark, and Joseph Peterson, *The Book of Oberon: A Sourcebook of Elizabethan Magic* (Woodbury, MN: Llewelyn Publications, 2015)

Kelly, Edmund, *The Grand Grimoire, Red Dragon* (Morrisville, NC: Lulu Press, Inc., 2019)

Kelly, Edmund, *The Grimoire of St. Cyprian – English Edition* (Morrisville, NC: Press, Inc., 2019)

Laurence, Richard, *The Book of Enoch the Prophet* (Mecosta, MI: Wizards Bookshelf, 1976)

Le Véritable Dragon Noir: Ou les Forces Infernales soumises à l'homme (Brossard, QC: Editions Unicursal, 2017)

Leitao, Jose, *The Book of St. Cyprian: The Sorcerer's Treasure* (France: Hadean Press, 2014)

Levi, Eliphas, *Transcendental Magic: Its Doctrine and Ritual*, trans. by A.E. Waite (London: George Redway Publications, 1896)

MacDonald, Michael-Albion, *Secret of Secrets: The Unwritten Mysteries of Esoteric Qabbalah* (Gillette, NJ: Heptangle Books, 1986)

Maggi, Humberto, *The Book of St. Cyprian: The Great Book of True Magic* (Charlotte, NC: Nephilim Press, 2018)

Peterson, Joseph, *Grimorium Verum* (CreateSpace Independent Publishing Platform, 2007)

Pope Leo III (attributed), *Enchiridion Leonis papæ* (Lyon, France: 1601)

Skinner, Stephen, and David Rankine, *The Grimoire of St. Cyprian: Clavis Inferni*, Sourceworks of Ceremonial Magic, 5 (Singapore: Golden Hoard Press, 2017)

Skinner, Stephen, and David Rankine, *The Veritable Key of Solomon*, Sourceworks of Ceremonial Magic, 4 (Singapore: Golden Hoard Press, 2013)

Stratton-Kent, Jake, *The Testament of Cyprian the Mage*, Encyclopaedia Goetica, 3 (London: Scarlet Imprint, 2014)

Sufurino, Jonas, *El Libro de San Cipriano*, trans. by Moorne (Buenos Aires: Maucci Publishing, 1910)

Sufurino, Jonas, *El Libro de San Cipriano*, trans. by Moorne (Editorial Verbum, 2020)

Sufurino, Jonas, *El Libro Inferno*, trans. by Moorne (Buenos Aires: Maucci Publishing, 1910)

Sufurino, Jonas, *La Magia Suprema de Jonás Sufurino*, ed. by Angel Rodriguez (San Juan: Editorial Nuevo Mundo, 2019)

Sufurino, Jonas, *La Magia Suprema Negro, Roja, E Inferna*, trans. by Moorne (Rome: A. Ward: 1916)

www.ingramcontent.com/pod-product-compliance
Lightning Source LLC
Chambersburg PA
CBHW021232090426
42740CB00006B/491